R Benjamin Jenson

FIRST WAYNE STREET
UNITED METHODIST CHURCH
300 East Wayne
Fort Wayne, Indiana 46802

THE SACRAMENTS

an experiment
in ecumenical honesty

THE SACRAMENTS
an experiment
in ecumenical honesty

[
ERNEST J. FIEDLER
R. BENJAMIN GARRISON
]

abingdon press/nashville and new york
fides publishers, inc./notre dame, indiana

Scripture quotations unless otherwise noted are from the Revised Standard Version of the Bible, copyrighted 1946 and 1952 by the Division of Christian Education, National Council of Churches, and are used by permission.

Scripture quotations noted *The Jerusalem Bible* are from *The New Testament of the Jerusalem Bible,* copyright 1969 by Doubleday & Company, Inc.

Scripture quotations noted *Good News for Modern Man* are from *The New Testament in Today's English Version,* copyright 1967 by American Bible Society, New York.

Quotations of "Four Quartets" from *The Complete Poems and Plays* by T. S. Eliot, published by Harcourt, Brace & World, Inc. in 1952, are used by permission of Harcourt, Brace & World, Inc. and Faber and Faber Ltd.

Quotations from *Claimed by God for Mission* by Eugene Stockwell, published by World Outlook Press in 1965, are used by permission of Board of Missions of The United Methodist Church, New York.

SET UP, PRINTED, AND BOUND BY
THE PARTHENON PRESS, AT NASHVILLE,
TENNESSEE, UNITED STATES OF AMERICA

TO THE PEOPLE OF GOD
IN EVERY PLACE
CALLED TO WITNESS
TO HIS LOVE AND GRACE

ESPECIALLY THOSE OF
THE CHURCH OF THE SACRED HEART
WARRENSBURG, MISSOURI
AND OF
THE WESLEY UNITED METHODIST CHURCH
URBANA-CHAMPAIGN, ILLINOIS

STUMBLING PILGRIMS
WHOM WE TWO STAMMERING
WOULD-BE PROPHETS
LOVE IN THE LORD

[preface]

The opportunity to project these pages came in an invitation to present them in conjunction with the Willson Lectures at Southwestern University, Georgetown, Texas, during the summer of 1968. The request to attempt the project in tandem was more than two good friends and ecumenical enthusiasts cared to resist. We gladly record here our gratitude to President Durwood Fleming and to those in attendance at that summer's Texas Methodist Pastor's School.

What we have written here is not intended primarily for scholars. Rather, we have tried to address working pastors and concerned laymen, Catholic and Protestant, who wish to rethink the significance of the sacraments in terms of the principles of antiquity and the priorities of modernity.

We have had the help of many people and of several groups, some of whom are named herein and hereafter. We wish, however, to name in particular these who have generously given specific assistance: Dr. Herbert Eschliman, Chairman of the Department of English at Central Missouri State College, who read the Fiedler chapters (2, 4, 6, 8, and 10); Mrs. Raymond Knell and Mrs. Ingvar Schousboe, who perused the Garrison chapters (1, 3, 5, 7, and 9); Mrs. Donald Alberts and Mrs. Marie McMillan, who prepared the typescript; also Miss Gail Clair who compiled the index.

Years ago John Wesley was asking, "Though we cannot think alike, may we not love alike?" The answer is self-evidently affirmative. Moreover, as we have discovered and attempted herein to show, we think a good deal more alike than we had guessed before we stopped to listen and to share.

We undertook this project with combined enthusiasm and hesitation. But we are better pastor-priests because the enthusiasm took command of the hesitation. We send forth this book with the prayerful hope that our readers will find the published result to be rational, faithful, and helpful.

ERNEST J. FIEDLER
R. BENJAMIN GARRISON

[contents]

[1]

MAN'S SACRAMENTAL
STARTING POINT

We have deliberately chosen to begin with man in this analysis of the creative use of the sacraments in the modern church. The sacraments are, after all, for man. They are *from God*, but their thrust and intent, their institution and result, are for *man*.

Objections to this procedure are probably not generically dissimilar to the familiar plaint that, when men talk about God, they are using anthropocentric language. The ancient Greeks used to observe with some glee that, if the cows had a God, they would picture that deity with hooves and horns. The appropriate reply is that of course man uses anthropocentric language. That accusation amounts to little more than a tautology, translating out as: man uses human language. Such information can hardly be termed intellectually startling. Unless a man is an angel (very few of us qualify) he has no other language to use.

Similarly, since we have no way to plug into some divine circuitry, we must begin this discussion of sacramental the-

11

ology from where we stand. Subsequently we shall make what we firmly take to be defensible inferences about how the sacraments fit into the plan of God (we shall even undertake to defend these inferences), but meanwhile we must be content with "telling it like it is" from man's admittedly limited and liable perspective.

I

Man's sacramental starting point is his own need. No catalog of human needs can be anything like complete (anymore than can any conceivable catalog of his virtues), but chief among them, it seems to us, are these:

First is *the human need for cleansing.* All the way from the primitive, probably prehistoric exorcisms performed by our forefathers around mystic campfires, campfires lighted by the flint and spark of deified lightning from an alien sky, to Isaiah in the Temple woefully crying out for cleansing, to modern man who may disdain religion but wouldn't for anything miss the daily *"lavabo me"* of his shower bath, man expresses the need to be cleaned up, purified. The sacraments are the apparent end terms, or climax, in such a series of aspirations.

The sacraments also express *the need for wholeness.* The word "sin" is not at all a pretty one, but that is only because it describes a very ugly fact. We are the creatures who are able to stand yet likely to fall. We are the beings who consistently choose our own interests when given the merest excuse and, by that very choosing, fracture our own real interests. We are the ones who camouflage our failures, exaggerate our virtues, and try to escape the consequences of both. In short, we are the only creatures who are able to subtract sums from our own nature. A horse can be nothing except a horse. If he cheats at the Kentucky Derby, that cheating has not been done *by* him but *to* him. A man, on the other hand, can be less than a man. That is the story of our lives. We stand in desperate and sometimes despairing need of wholeness. From that fact the sacraments take their starting point.

Since man is fractured or less than himself, it then follows that another way to say the same thing is that *man needs manhood*. He seeks himself, yet—and at the same time—flees from himself. He is not quite free enough to be independent and not quite obedient enough to be free. Like a sheep in a snowstorm eating its own wool, he keeps plucking at the stuff of his own humanity, diminishing and devouring it beyond recovery—on his own.

The need for men to recover their wholeness has been historically focused by Christian theology in the experience of forgiveness. In this, as in so many other important regards, theology is what Edwin Lewis used to call "the elucidation of experience." The sometimes rigorously formal doctrines of penance and atonement are but (sometimes) stylized expressions of the human experience of brokenhearted regret and the need to be rid of it and the need to be whole again. This need has been expressed limpingly (the totem pole), awfully (Isaiah in the Temple), or—for Christians—perfectly (the Cross). Nevertheless, the need is real.

The meeting of that need, in the Judeo-Christian context, is what is meant by forgiveness. For those who stand in that historical lineage, forgiveness is *fore-forgiveness*. Our present experience of it is based upon and bonded by the prior fact of it. It has already been given.

Carl Michalson used to reply to the "When were you saved, brother?" query with the rejoinder, "In A.D. 29" (apparently quoting a nineteenth-century German pastor).

Beneath that deceptively flip reply was an almost nonchalant confidence. It wasn't really nonchalant, of course. It justified no brash and careless antinomianism.[1] What it does justify is humble acceptance of the prior and continued great-heartedness of God, overmatching the prior and often continued self-preference of man. The man who prefers himself; God who gives himself; the man who accepts both—these are the facets of forgiveness.

Of this forgiveness, Edward Schillebeeckx, the distinguished Dutch scholar, has observed: "Although forgiveness can be realized instantaneously, it nevertheless allows of a subsequent process by which holiness steadily takes possession of and re-forms the whole psychological make-up of the convert."[2]

Although that comes from the pen of a Roman Catholic theologian, its source could easily have been a Protestant. Notably, a Methodist might note, it could have been phrased by John Wesley, who thought of the forgiven life in Christ as an event followed by a process. The event is the experience of wholeness; the process is the fleshing out of the event.

Perhaps a Protestant may also be permitted to observe that we have been guilty of sundering the event from the process. Some of us, in our modern sophistication, have made do with a rather impressive process which, nonetheless, centers in no event—in no soul-wrenching, heart-changing, God-flung act. Others of us, in our conservative simplicity, have made do with an authentic event from which nothing flows except stale and aging memories. "Salvation" or "wholeness" (equally good

[1] Literally anti-law: anti (against) *nomos* (law). In ecclesiastical history the antinomian is one who holds that, because of the act and fact of Christ, nothing more is required of the Christian. Faith is everything; good and evil deeds are equally unimportant.
[2] *Christ the Sacrament of the Encounter with God* (New York: Sheed & Ward, 1963), p. 136.

14

and, in biblical terms, nearly equivalent words) is the whole work of God, not just the beginning of it.

Probably some of the resistance to and impatience with what Schillebeeckx (and Christian theology generally) means by "instantaneously" is an ambiguity almost inherent in the word. The instant, or the "moment in time" as biblical Christianity understands the term, is not marked off by a tick on one's watch but by an insight or an exhilaration in one's life. When the young lover exclaims, "That was the time!" he does not mean "it was midnight," but "she kissed me!" Just so, time—the moment—in the New Testament is not *chronos* (clock time) but *kairos* (full time, filled time, time with a qualitative punch to it). "But when the fullness of the time was come, God sent forth his Son" (Gal. 4:4 KJV). "And when the day of Pentecost was fully come" (Acts 2:1 KJV). "And last of all he was seen of me also, as of one born out of due time" (I Cor. 15:8 KJV). "Time was" becomes "time is" when, as Schillebeeckx helps us see, the "elements of human life become *kairoi*; that is, becoming saving moments." [3]

Another of man's needs, we would contend, is *for mystery.* At least he is always and inevitably confronted with it. Mystery is literally the "close-mouthed." It will not tell us of itself. But the church's sacraments *try* to give a kind of enacted articulation to the pondered impenetrabilities which characterize our existence. They "speak out" or "act out" the mystery of a man's history. Life's authentic events—birth and death and all that is bracketed between—are mysteriously but undeniably beyond our control.

Still another of man's needs, embodied in his sacramental starting point, is *his need for presence.*

[3] *Ibid.*, p. 177.

15

The term "presence" as used here seems, strangely, both vague and exact. It appears vague because it reminds us of intimations of the spirit world, of what the old Scots called "ghoulies and ghosties, and things that go bump in the night." But it is exact because it too refers specifically to event. If sacramental theology means anything (and of course we believe it does, else we would not be writing this book), it means that Christ is really present in these frail and fateful deeds bracketed by bread and wine, water, oil, gesture, word, and song.

Hence and (since Christ) henceforth man's need is for a *presence received in Christ.* As we shall see in the chapters on the Eucharist, this need is sacramentally central. This is the pivotal point of Schillebeeckx's book, or so at least it seemed to a Protestant. Thus he says, "The man Jesus, as the personal visible realization of the divine grace of redemption, is *the* sacrament, the primordial sacrament." [4] All the other sacraments (the traditional ones) are such only because they manifest the presence of him who is *the* sacrament. Whether we number the "official" sacraments at two or seven or somewhere in between or more, "each . . . is thus a particular kind of encounter with Christ." [5] Baptism is death to self in his presence. Confirmation is the celebration of the new life in his presence arising from that death. The Eucharist is the manifestation of that presence in its most cherished sacramental mode. Penance is confession to Christ who is present. Holy Matrimony is the deepest and most intimate presence of human with human, sanctified by him who was present at the marriage in Cana of Galilee and now graciously present in this one. Holy Orders involve service which is judged and justified, or judged and condemned, according as

[4] *Ibid.,* p. 15.   [5] *Ibid.,* p. 115.

16

it shows forth the Lord's presence. Extreme Unction is meant to send forth the mortal soul with an immortal presence.

Man's need is also for a presence not only received but given.

Sometimes this is given in words. The words "thank you" may mean, "You were with me in my need and identified yourself with me." The words "I am sorry" mean, "I was *not* with you in your need and am smitten by my failure." The words "I love you" assert that life is constituted by presence and that, until that fact is lived with, existence is not really and presently alive. Words provide channels for presence and minister to our need for it.

At other times man's need for a presence which he gives is expressed not in words but in telling gestures, in both senses of the qualifier "telling": (1) gestures which tell, announce, or proclaim; (2) gestures which are decisive or crucial, as in the value judgment, "Lincoln's Emancipation Proclamation was a telling event in American history." In the first sense, the proclamatory gesture may be illustrated by the handshake. Try conveying the impression of virility, strength, or support with a limp handshake! In the second sense, the decisive gesture is illustrated by walking a picket line: The decisive gesture puts your body where your life is. To anticipate some chapters to follow: The Eucharist is a form of sacramental gesturing which is both proclamatory and decisive (that is why it is both enervating and unhistorical to omit from the liturgy the "manual acts," the actual breaking of the bread, the visible lifting of the cup). More largely, the total act of the Eucharist is such double-sided gesture: It proclaims the Lord's death ("this is my body broken"); it is decisive in shaming what is divisive in today's church ("all of you drink of it").

17

When one makes a gift it is to establish a presence, unless that gift is a meaningless gesture (to employ our earlier analogy). When an elder of my family passed on to me the family Bible in which are some biographical entries nearly two centuries old, it was to make present to me and for me the whole complex of human frailty and faith, of hope realized or cut short, which go to make up my family's self-understanding, life, and work. When I give a woman an engagement ring, it is to present *myself* to her. With that understood, I could have given her instead a chunk of coal set in a piece of tin (not to be recommended but nevertheless possible!). If I send flowers to a bereaved friend, it is to share his grief and bear his sorrow as present with him.

Once more, our sacraments are centered in *the need for community*. So while the import and meaning of a sacrament is personal, it is never exclusively individual. Indeed the very concept of the individual is nonsense except as over against and in the midst of a community of persons.

It would appear at least to the Protestant partner in this authorship that the Roman Catholic practice of the sacrament of penance (in distinction to what the church has tried to teach) has been too individualistic and subjective. The priest who binds and looses does so in the name of God but also in the name and for the sake of the community in which both he and the penitent are set. The penitent has set himself, in his sins, against the well-being and integrity of the community. To neglect or gloss over that fact is to subordinate and perhaps to subjugate one of the human being's primary needs.

Finally, man's sacraments arise from his *need for celebration*. An analogy may be helpful. When a married couple celebrates a wedding anniversary, several elements are inter-

18

mixed: (1) gratefully looking back upon a supremely important event in their lives; (2) expectantly looking forward to new meaning and joys arising from that event; (3) freely rededicating themselves, their souls and bodies, to those values and duties which, taken together, have given them something to celebrate today.

This illustration may be a bit too chummy, but it does help indicate how Christian worship, when genuine, and especially sacramental worship, has above it the banner lead line: "CELEBRATION!" Significantly a recent study in Christian worship is entitled, *The Celebration of the Gospel*. In celebrating worship (the phrase is almost a redundancy), (1) we gratefully look back upon a victory called, in theological shorthand, "the Christ Event"; (2) we expectantly look forward to those new things God intends to say to us and accomplish in us; (3) we freely rededicate ourselves, our souls and bodies, to those values and duties which, taken together, give us something to celebrate today.

No wonder the scriptures so often exhort us to rejoice. "This kind of confidence in God's grace," as Luther reminds us, "makes us joyful, high-spirited, and eager in our relations with God and with all mankind." [6] The springs of our gladness are deeper than the wells of our sadness.

II

It would be possible (though not, at this point in our effort, profitable) to go back through the foregoing catalog of man's needs to see how they are addressed by the various

---

[6] From *Reformation Writings of Martin Luther*, trans. with introduction and notes from the definitive Weimar ed. by Bertram Lew Woolf (London: Lutterworth Press, 1956), II, 288-89.

sacraments. That would, however, anticipate more detailed discussion to follow.

It may be helpful, though by way of anticipation, to summarize these human yearnings as they relate to the sacral acts which have emerged in the life of the church under the force of the gospel. The relationship is in some cases obvious, needing only to be stated, not elaborated upon. Man's need for cleansing is principally dramatized in penance, to a lesser extent in extreme unction. Father Fiedler may wish to insist in Chap. IV that baptism should be included here.

The Protestant corrective need not, I think, argue with this substantially. The doctrine of original sin is not the perverse product of theology's dark imagination. It is an intellectual formulation of a fact. Man does betray an inevitable tendency to become entangled with himself. He is, as we have said, pridefully bent upon self-preference. There is no use denying it.

Nevertheless, baptism is also and at the same time, and in my judgment emphatically, a communal sacrament. It sets the individual's life within that of a community. Infant baptism in particular sets young feet on the path of The Way, turns the young face toward Jesus and, as Arthur John Gossip put it, makes Jesus a great fact for him which he can never long escape or ignore. Indeed, all the sacraments are corporate before they are individual, corporate as the price of their being individual.

Furthermore, our need for presence and for mystery is ministered to by holy communion and by holy matrimony. All these are acts of celebration. We speak of "celebrating the Eucharist," but all the sacraments should be celebrated, exalted in, lifted up, with a kind of holy hilarity. The full round of man's needs, from birth to death, from rebirth to new life, are overlaid by that mysterious mosaic which we call man's sacramental life.

III

As a kind of bridge to and partial anticipation of Father Fiedler's observations in Chap. II, about "God's Sacramental Starting Point," I wish to conclude this chapter with some summary of, and comment upon, the late archbishop William Temple's notion of "The Sacramental Universe." [7] One need not share the great Anglican's confidence about the possibility of a Christian metaphysic, or even of a Christian ontology, in order to sense the seminal nature of his contributions to sacramental thought. One might note parenthetically that the archbishop himself seemed to sense this. In the above cited chapter, he writes: "The thought seems tangled. Yet I believe it is only because we are attempting the inevitable, yet impossible task of expressing in conceptual terms what is nothing less than life itself."

Note: "impossible" but "inevitable." Let us then make an effort, although in necessarily the tersest of terms.

By the term "sacramental universe," Temple asserts

the supremacy and absolute freedom of God; the reality of the physical world and its process as His Creation; the vital signifi-cance of the material and temporal world to the Eternal Spirit; and the spiritual issue of the process of the finite and time-enduring spirits in the infinite and eternal Spirit. [And now the controlling sentence:] matter . . . is created by spirit . . . to be the vehicle of spirit's self-realization.

[7] *Nature, Man and God* (New York: The Macmillan Co., 1949), chap. 19; see esp. pp. 493-95.

It is in this context that we are to understand Temple's otherwise enigmatic statement that "Christianity . . . is the most avowedly materialist of all the great religions." The Christian interpretation-proclamation of the Christ Event as "the Word made flesh" is the particularizing of this universal principle. Temple takes the universe, in the literal sense, with high seriousness and presses us back with vigor upon both its "material" and its "spiritual" components. Neither can be understood nor can even exist without the other. That may be denied, but even its denial is an act of faith.

Yet it is the conviction that reality is essentially sacramental, two-sided, and interactive, which leads Temple to make his famous statement on worship—a statement which amounts almost to *skandalon* to some modern presuppositions. Having stated elsewhere that the world can be saved from chaos by nothing except worship, Temple now tells us what he means by worship: "To worship is to quicken the conscience by the holiness of God, to feed the mind with the truth of God, to purge the imagination by the beauty of God, to open the heart to the love of God, to devote the will to the purpose of God." [8]

Recognizing that the term sacrament encompasses a wide difference of meaning, Temple nevertheless insists that the sacramental principle is capable of uniting the most viable of these: ground and consequence, thought and expression, goal and instrument. The sacraments are thus ecclesiastical only because they are participants in a reality that goes before and runs beyond the church. Though they are, in conventional vocabulary, the outward and visible signs of an inward and spiritual grace, and though to Christians they are inex-

[8] *The Hope of a New World* (New York: The Macmillan Co., 1923), p. 30.

22

pressibly dear, they possess no sacramental squatter's rights. The whole wide world *is* in his hand and expressive of his creative power and finesse.

Nevertheless, sacraments are not mere psychological inducements to a state of mind. They really convey what is real. Not inevitably—man's freedom is factual, sometimes fatally so. God never thrusts his gifts upon us, as Temple observes elsewhere. Nevertheless both the conveyance and what is conveyed is real and neither can be known, even imperfectly, without the other.

We have been using (perhaps even bandying about) terms like reality, freedom, spirit, material, grace, power. Any sophomore in philosophy (indeed any reasonably thoughtful human being) knows that many of these terms have shifted radically, even reversed, across the centuries. As we shall see in Chapts. V and VI, the term "real presence" had a meaning for the medievals which is hardly immediately clear to moderns. No matter. What Temple is struggling to express is that what is conveyed in a sacramental universe is not "things" (grace or the like) but God himself. Everything turns on the factuality of this faith.

It is out of our certitude about this—proclaimed and explored, wondered at and thought about—that we have projected this book. Man's sacramental starting point is ever available to him and forever beyond him. Here, for the moment, we must be content to let the matter rest.

23

[2]

GOD'S SACRAMENTAL
STARTING POINT

The mysterious prologue to John's account of the life of Jesus from its outset directs attention to what might be called God's sacramental starting point. Commentators have long noted that John's Gospel begins with an effort to hinge the whole account of Christ's earthly life and mission on its eternal pre-creation essence. In his brief collection of words, John would have us consider, as far as we are able, Christ's life in the essence he already and always shared with the Father and the Spirit:

> In the *beginning* was the *Word*:
> the Word was with God
> and the Word *was God*.
> He was *with God* in the beginning.
> Through him all *things* came to be,
> *not one thing* had its being but through him.
> All that came to be had life in him
> and that life was the light of men,

> a light that shines in the dark,
> a light that darkness could not overpower.
>
> The Word was the true light
> that enlightens all men;
> and *he was coming into the world.*
> He *was in* the world
> that had its being through him,
> and the world *did not know* him.
> He came to his own domain
> and his own people did not accept him.
> But *to all who did* accept him
> he gave power to become *children of God,*
> to all who believe in the name of him
> who was born not out of human stock
> or urge of the flesh
> or will of man
> but of God himself.
> *The Word was made flesh,*
> *he lived among us,*
> *and we saw his glory,*
> the glory that is his as the only Son of the Father,
> full of grace and truth.
>
> No one has ever seen God;
> it is the only Son, who is nearest to the Father's heart,
> who has made him known. (John 1:1-5, 9-14, 18.) [1]

He speaks of the "Word" and then tells us that this word was spoken temporally. To talk of "words" is already to deal with one of the means utilized in the making of sacraments.

It would be interesting at this point to digress and study John's entire Gospel vis-à-vis sacraments. But it would, in

[1] *The Jerusalem Bible* (Garden City, N. Y.: Doubleday & Co., 1966). Italics mine.

the time and space available to us, amount more to an unwarranted digression than a contribution. However, a remark or two are hopefully acceptable.

One of the investigations of note on this point is the learned and highly esteemed study of the Fourth Gospel by C. H. Dodd [2] which emphasizes the sign and symbol stress of this Gospel. In fact, Dodd goes so far as to call it "The Book of Signs." I am inclined to suggest that we accept the fact of the strong sacramental underpinning of John's insights and proceed from that perspective. It is easy to nitpick the academics of such a subject to the point that it becomes a kind of game. The agreement-disagreement factors here cross denominational lines quite ecumenically. If you are interested in pursuing the matter a bit further, I would suggest Bruce Vawter's contribution of a decade ago summarized in "The Johannine Sacramentary" [3] and the commentaries of Raymond E. Brown in the ecumenically blessed effort of the Anchor Bible[4] as primary sources.

Roughly summarizing the contents of these considerations and adding personal thoughts, I might say simply that man uses words and actions to communicate. These he produces with his body. As a matter of fact, the only means of communication that man possesses is his human body. (Even "ESP" depends radically on the body.) From this perspective the surpassing generosity of the incarnation can be seen from a slightly different point of view than is normally discussed in the journals of theology. With the incarnation, *God* takes

[2] *The Interpretation of the Fourth Gospel* (London: Cambridge University Press, 1953).

[3] *Theology Digest*, VI (Winter, 1958).

[4] *The Gospel According to John* (I-XII) in "The Anchor Bible" (Garden City, N.Y.: Doubleday & Co., 1966).

a human body. He now communicates with man in the manner that is normal to *man*.

How well he succeeded, how completely tangible he became with a human body, John expresses in another of his writings:

> We write to you about the Word of life, which has existed from the very beginning: we have *heard* it, and we have *seen* it with our eyes; yes, we have *seen* it, and our hands have *touched* it. When this life became *visible*, we *saw* it; so we speak of it and tell you about the eternal life which was with the Father and was made known to us.
>
> What we have seen and heard we tell to you also, so that you will join with us in the fellowship that we have with the Father and with his Son Jesus Christ. We write this in order that our joy may be complete. (I John 1:1-4.) [5]

In many ways it seems presumptous to write further, unless one possessed the pioneering theological talents and insights of a modern prophet like Teilhard de Chardin. But we must reject the temptation to stop and accept the presumptous effort of continuing.

One amalgamation of the concepts of sacraments and communication is the following:

> We shall see in John a strong emphasis on events in Christ's life which foreshadow the sacramental life of the Church. John is dealing with a Christian audience which already depends on baptism for its life and the Eucharist for nourishment of the life. The only information in the Synoptics on baptism is a verse commanding it (Mt. 28:19), and on the Eucharist, the verses

[5] *Good News for Modern Man* (New York: American Bible Society, 1967). Italics mine.

instituting it (Mt. 14:22-24). John takes these institutions for granted, not even mentioning them, but gives the rich background and meaning of baptism in references to the living water of rebirth in cc. 3, 4, 7, 13, and of the Eucharist in the discourse on the living bread in c. 6, and in references to the vine of the new dispensation in cc. 2, 15. John shows the ultimate source of both sacraments in 19:34.[6]

A lengthy history of God's more indirect revelation and man's painfully difficult efforts both to understand and communicate with him in return are recorded in the Old Testament. The New Testament, then, seems to demonstrate that the exchange can now be carried on in a manner natural to man, that is, by means of the body. As Schillebeeckx has said: "The human encounter with Jesus is therefore the sacrament of the encounter with God." [7] This happens with every event and at each moment of Christ's life, but especially does it assume importance in the great events of his redemptive death, resurrection, and ascension. Even this, however, is not yet all. Christ makes his presence among us permanently active and permanently tangible by establishing the church as his continuing bodily presence. This he provides for man living in the ages after the catalyst of his physical body is gone from man's direct physical encounter. Within this context we find the basis for any sacrament. Were this not so, the bodily communication factor of the incarnation would be lost to us. The II Vatican Council said:

> To accomplish so great a work *Christ is always present in His church,* especially in her liturgical celebrations. . . . By His

---

[6] "New Testament Reading Guide," No. 13, *Liturgical Press* (Collegeville, Minn., 1965).

[7] *Christ the Sacrament of the Encounter with God*, p. 15.

> power He is present in the sacraments, so that when a man
> baptizes it is really Christ Himself who baptizes. He is present
> in His word, since it is He Himself who speaks when the holy
> Scriptures are read in the church. He is present, finally, when
> the Church prays and sings, for He promised: "Where two or
> three are gathered together for my sake, there am I in the midst
> of them. (Italics mine.)[8]

An illustration of the continuity of body presence through
the sacraments can be seen in an interesting point made by
Schillebeeckx who wrote that not one of the twelve apostles
who had such immediate contact with Christ, the "primordial
sacrament," was baptized. But Paul, the "thirteenth apostle,"
who had not physically contacted the earthly Christ, was
baptized (Acts 9:18). Sacramentality would thus be seen
to bridge the gap between the glorified Christ and unglorified
humanity. It became operative as the entity we call "church"
after the ascension of Christ's physical, earthly body.

The Sacraments find their place in the larger context of
church as the necessary formative element of effective symbols that man needs even in his basic human life. Man
has used and has always needed symbols in his process of
communication. Situations and occasions inevitably arise
when words alone are unsuccessful or incomplete as the
means of communication. Even in very simple things, we
frequently find that a box of candy, flowers, an embrace,
a smile are more effective than words can be as a means
of communication. This problem of ineptness is in all language. It is not only true between individuals but also for
the communication of information and knowledge to and
between members of a community.

[8] *The Documents of Vatican II* (New York: The America Press
[Association Press], 1966), "Liturgy," No. 7, pp. 140-41.

Contemporary studies in linguistic analysis note that language seems inevitably and ultimately to lead to *mystery*, to depths whose expression cannot be accomplished with language alone. As language begins to reach this point, it begins to use vehicles like metaphors and poetry. But finally these too fail to express the greater depth of the human person. The point is reached when man's last device for communication is ritual. It is also his most basic device. Modern philosophy today may in fact be converging with theology on this point in an increasing awareness of the ultimate need for signs. Essentially, radically, these are sacraments.

Theologically speaking, both Protestantism and Roman Catholicism since the Reformation have come to the same rationalistic stance in the matter of linguistic formulation, and, in effect, the problems of religion, God and man, have been considered as adequately worked out and stated adequately. Theology produced exact formulas, expressing rigid doctrinal positions and implying that the truths were all safely capsulized.

Paradoxically the mechanics of the physical sciences grew more fluid than the mechanics of theology whose aim is to study *mystery*, utterly boundless mystery. And science, in its points of contact with theology, encountered such rigid and static formulas that science decided, understandably, that it did not need religion or a god so neatly indexed and tabulated. In such a situation the tragedy, if we may call it that, of a man like Sigmund Freud is a good example of the results. Religious and doctrinal statements, being static and out of tune with the situation of contemporary man and his greater existential depth, could only be considered an illusion by a man dealing with the new concepts of psychology and the mysteries of human depth he was discovering.

But science itself then began to fall victim to the same hazard. If language was insufficient, or various unknowns were encountered, science would simply develop a system of symbols and equations. Science also ultimately has ended up with cold, stratified, and impersonal formulas when it speaks of man. Man might be scientifically described in an equation. But while "A+B=Man" might give a concrete statement, such a formula clearly could not begin to plumb the depths of man's existential reality.

Now it seems that science and religion are converging again. They come to the same dead end when they attempt to use restricted formulas to express the person as a loving, knowing being. They come to the point where words and formulas are insufficient or useless, and both have ended up groping for something more. In effect, the search has led back again to mystery and the inadequacy of language to express it satisfactorily. It may sound quite facile, but it would seem that people always come to an end of words and to a need for sacraments.

If we have begun to learn a costly lesson, and to safeguard falling into the same mistakes again, these signs and symbols, these sacraments must be kept in a dynamic state. They must communicate truly, but in a living way. God may lead us, in Christ, to the use of basic symbols, but the church must assure the dynamism of their expression. We are just beginning to emerge, hopefully, from a long static stage in accepting this responsibility. We have been so busy defending our doctrinal formulas that we allowed sacraments and worship to petrify. Hopefully, however, God's sacramental starting point is on the verge of being more actively accepted by man again. If he succeeds, a rebirth of religious life in greater depth is eminent and inevitable.

A theological worry: Let us not judge that *our* sacramental action contributes anything to God as God. We will merely get hung up in another maze that might take several more centuries to unscramble. The danger of assuming, even unconsciously, that our actions in any way contribute anything to God is that we essentially tend to reverse the roles of God and man. Even when most perfectly celebrated by man, God's sacramental "starting point" is not enriched. St. Thomas Aquinas sounds quite "modern" at this point. He says, for example:

> In the payment of these bodily observances . . . we busy ourselves in paying attention to the things of God, not as though we were of service to Him, as is the case when we are said to tend, or cultivate, other things by our attentions, but because such actions are of service to ourselves, enabling us to come nearer to God. And because by inward acts we go straight to God, therefore it is by inward acts properly that we worship God: nevertheless outward acts also belong to the cult, or worship, of God, inasmuch as by such acts our mind is raised to God.[9]

> There are exercised on man certain sanctifications through some sensible things, which man is washed, or anointed, or given to eat or drink, with the utterance of sensible words . . . not indeed as though profitable to him (God).[10]

> We pay God honor and reverence, not for His sake (because He is of Himself full of glory to which no creature can add any-

---

[9] *Summa Contra Gentiles. Of God and His Creatures*, by Joseph Rickaby S. J. (Westminster, Maryland; Carroll Press, 1950); Lib. III, Cap. 119.

[10] *Summa Contra Gentiles*, III, 119.

thing), but for our own sake, because by the very fact that we revere and honor God, our mind is subject to Him; wherein its perfection consists, since a thing is perfected by being subjected to its superior, for instance the body is perfected by being quickened by the soul, and the air by being enlightened by the sun.[11]

God, therefore, is liberal to the highest degree, and He alone can properly be called liberal; for every other being, except Him, by acting acquires some good which is the end intended.[12]

So we receive. As we enact sacramental life in the church, we must receive constantly and even more consciously the sacramental starting and sustaining principle of the Father —and, of course, it is a living thing, a living presence, a Person. He gives, we receive; we *embody* his life. Hence the need to attend to the condition of our body—the church! As we learn to receive properly, we will be "giving" everything we can.

What is the extent of this giving by God to us? It is beyond any measuring available to us. It seems that it consists of nothing less than God himself. As Paul says with such undiluted, undiminishing, and absolute timeliness, "This hope does not disappoint us, for God has poured out his life into our hearts by means of the Holy Spirit, who is God's Gift to us!" His giving is as total as himself. The only modification, restriction, or abstraction is our own hesitancy, refusal, or temerity. He will not change. The only real question is—will we?

[11] *Summa Theologica*, II, 81, art. 2.
[12] *Summa Contra Gentiles*, I, 93, 7.

[3]

BAPTISM AS BIRTH

The church is a tower built upon a foundation of water. This proclamation by an early theologian of the post-apostolic church would not, one supposes, make much sense to many in the present-day church. It is not that the church is formed and defined by baptism in the more restricted meaning of this sacrament (although a limited case can be made out for that). It is rather that what Jesus was baptized into and involved in is *the* baptism beneath our baptisms. The baptism wherewith he was baptized is the base and bond for the baptism in which we are baptized.

And that is at once too subtle and too demanding to be readily grasped by many modern Christians. By them baptism is variously considered a name giving ceremony, a consecration of parenthood, a confession of faith, a public avowal, a private contract, a pleasant custom, or a historic but not terribly important form. To the extent that such misunderstandings exist and (worse) exist with the latitudenarian leave of a sacramentally lax church, we have, bluntly, departed from the New Testament, even when we read from it at baptismal

34

"ceremonies." And to that extent the authors reluctantly agree with a modern theologian's assertion that the contemporary practice of baptism can hardly be regarded as anything short of scandalous. His reference is to infant baptism, but (on this side of the Atlantic, at least) no such restriction quite applies.

The shape and content of this chapter and the following one are formed around the conviction that baptism, like the Christian life itself, is also an event followed by a process. Recall what was said in Chap. I about a similar dialectic found in and arising from the forgiven life in Christ. Recall, too, what was affirmed about the fore-giveness of forgiveness. Quite literally we *were* saved in A.D. 29. That is *the* event in which our consequent baptisms participate as satellite events. That baptism is the drama in which our baptisms are episodes.

Subordinately and derivatively understood, the rite of Christian baptism may legitimately be said to be an event ("baptism as birth") as well as a process ("baptism as life").

In such birth and throughout such life God is the Father. Nothing we can defiantly try to abrogate our sonship can in any way destroy that fatherhood. *We cannot even sin our way out!* As one of our baptismal liturgies phrases it: "Dearly beloved, for as much as all men are heirs of life eternal and subjects of the saving grace, . . . I beseech you to call upon God the Father. . . ." The difference between Christians and other men is not so much that Christians are baptized but others are not. The difference is that Christians declare, in their special and specific baptism, that they know all men have been baptized "from the foundation of the world."

The great and overarching fact that validates baptism is the great and overarching fact about God, namely, that he is

35

Father of every creature who ever drew breath, and therefore each one of us is his child. *"For God so loved the world"*: not the Christian world only, not the penitent world exclusively, but all the world.

This is difficult for us to accept, just as it was hard for the professionally religious of Jesus' time to understand. They were consternated when he displayed that love toward a woman of the streets. They were confused when he included in that love men who darkened the door of the Jewish church only when they wanted to beg. They were insanely angered when he portrayed that love by saying a heretical foreigner, a Samaritan by birth, demonstrated this love more thoroughly than did all the multiform self-righteousness of Judaism.

I

When baptism, whether cosmic or personal, is thus understood, many of the arguments about infant baptism seem sterile and settled (though we harbor no illusions that our saying so will in fact settle them!).

What is commonly not understood is that the disputes about baptism (infant and/or adult, for instance) really rest upon differing conceptions of faith.[1] Where faith is (mis-) understood as deriving from the competence of the individual, that is, where faith is the result of a man's volition and the fruit of his mind, quite naturally adult baptism is regarded as necessarily normative. If, on the other hand, faith is seen as kindred of trust, whose affirmation is closer to "you love me" than it is to "I believe in you" or even to "I love you," then infant baptism is the appropriate mode. Either way, it is wise to recognize that the issue is joined at the collision

[1] Cf. Martin E. Marty, *Baptism* (Philadelphia: Fortress Press [Muhlenberg Press], 1962), pp. 44-45.

point of differing concepts of faith rather than at the point of some intrinsically superior, or inferior, doctrine of baptism.

We opt for the latter concept of faith, and therefore hold that infant baptism is properly understood as the basic form of this basic sacrament. More will be said later, briefly, about the tenuous scriptural data for settling the argument either way in terms of specifics. But the larger biblical design for faith, which speaks of God who seeks and of men who, in his sight and presence, are infants even if they are adults —all this is weighty argument for understanding infant baptism as normative not accidental, central not marginal. As James F. White has written in *The Worldliness of Worship*, baptism "is not a reward for faith, . . . it is not for us to prove our acceptability, not to demonstrate our merit, not to deserve baptism."[2] In short, an exclusive emphasis upon so-called "believer's baptism" comes dangerously close to a doctrine of salvation by works.

To the familiar complaint that a person has a right to be asked whether he wants to be baptized, it may be sufficient to observe that nobody asks to be born either. This, to be sure, is argument by analogy, but the analogy goes to the center of the issue. What is at issue is precisely the given nature of our lives, and that is a prior fact which we cannot destroy. We may affirm it or deny it, but we cannot change it.

It was out of some such understanding of baptism as birth that Wesley reasoned for infant baptism. He agreed that it was difficult if not impossible to comprehend *how* baptism benefited the infant. But he contended, insightfully, that it is just as incomprehensible how the adult is brought again

[2] *The Worldliness of Worship* (New York: Oxford University Press, 1967), p. 146.

37

to birth in baptism. No one can arrange to be born. So, as Carl Michalson argued, "It is artificial to delay what is implicit from one's birth. . . ." [3] Baptism, he continued, is "the act in which the Church renews God's pledge." [4]

One more argument against limiting baptism to adults may be noted. The argument is admittedly somewhat negative. Nevertheless, it seems to us the latter constriction in the faith and practice of the church signals a loss of the sense of the corporateness of the Christian life, thus belying and denying one of the individual's elemental needs (namely, for community). This leads us to a discussion of the social or corporate nature of birth-in-baptism.

What I have here written is not addressed to, or even intended to be a part of, the extended debate of the centuries as to whether the New Testament authorized the baptism of infants. We are told in the Great Commission, Christ's last words to his disciples, to go "into all the world baptizing." The New Testament records more than one instance of a man *and his entire household* being baptized. (Acts 16:15; I Cor. 1:16.) The Bible does not explicitly prohibit the practice; the early church is known to have engaged in it. There are, however, as we have tried to show, more indicative arguments than those which can be induced by even an instructed biblicism.

II

Godfrey Dieckmann has vividly expressed the communality of baptism when he says that in this sacrament "the community of the faithful [is] going bond, as it were, for the

[3] *The Role of the Word in the Sacrament of Baptism,* unpublished paper, p. 3.
[4] *Ibid.,* p. 4.

new member of the community." [5] This is, or ought to be, true of the entire community. Even in infant baptism the parents or sponsors are present in their representative, not alone in their personal, capacity.

In baptism, then, the community is both witnessing a birth and affirming its own important responsibility for the shape and destiny of the consequent life (see Chap. IV). Baptism is the church's communal pronouncement that what God once did he continues to do, that his promises are sure, and that his power is present. Baptism dramatizes the church's humble confidence that he will do these things through this particular community.

It is because of the social or corporate core of baptism that the Reformation traditions in the large, and Roman Catholicism increasingly, have insisted that the rite should be celebrated in the presence of the worshiping congregation. Baptism is not a private pact but a public declaration and, religiously understood, a public trust. Thus Robert McAfee Brown has likened a baptism without a congregation to a sermon without hearers.[6] He is right. In baptism, as in all Christian worship, the church gathers to affirm and proclaim. The content of the affirmation and the point of the proclamation are the community's concern.

D. M. Baillie's characteristically able study, *The Theology of the Sacraments*, winsomely expresses this aspect of the life of the caring, sharing community. The great Scot writes:

There must be a real and important difference between the environment given to a child by a Church which takes infant

[5] *Come, Let Us Worship* (Garden City, N. Y. Image Books, 1966), p. 72.
[6] *The Significance of the Church* (Philadelphia: Westminster Press, 1956), p. 77.

39

baptism seriously and the environment given by a Church which denies this sacrament to infants. A Church which practices infant baptism with real belief and understanding inevitably has an attitude to its children which makes it in a peculiar sense a means of grace to them; and every time the sacrament is administered to an infant "in the face of the congregation" the Church and especially the parents are brought afresh to that attitude. In such a Church a child is indeed brought through baptism into a new . . . environment.[7]

Baillie does not spell out just what differences such an environment would stress. One supposes that such a community's forms of worship would be flexible and adapted to the needs and capacities of the youngest as well as the eldest; that its educational life would help equip the parents to interpret the drama of salvation, as Jesus did, in those homey terms which the childlike heart, of whatever age, can grasp and grow toward; that the church would, to put the same thing another way, refuse to be *in loco parentis*; that it would embody a quality of life which children could sense and share long before they could understand and articulate the presence of Christ. Anyway, as Baillie claims, in such a Church a child is brought through baptism into new birth.

To change the figure, the baptized life is not only one in which the twig is bent (parents, society at large, can do that) but one onto which the twig is grafted. You will recall that apt and potent figure which the apostle Paul uses to describe the church. The church, he says, is the body of Christ, and all of us are members of that body. That is simply profound and profoundly simple; a hand's power does not lie

[7] *The Theology of the Sacraments* (New York: Charles Scribner's Sons, 1957), pp. 87-88.

hidden in itself. The secret of the power of the hand is that it is attached to an arm. So, too, with life's power. The secret of man's power, the real secret of his dignity, is what he is attached to. In holy baptism the Christian community is saying that, insofar as it can influence man's life, his life will be procured in, judged by, and used through the church which is the body of Christ.

I presume that one reason that Paul said this, was his being a Jew. The Jew, of all men, knew that life is knit with life. The promise of God was given to Israel; not to any individual Israelite, however brilliant or spiritually perceptive he might have been. Paul came from and spoke to a people who knew that God's will is declared *to a people,* though it might require an individual prophet to made it clear. For the Hebrew's very starting point was, "Hear, O Israel: The Lord our God is one Lord. . . . And you shall teach them diligently to your children." This Paul understood. So he was able to say that the church is a social organism which shows forth Christ's power.

III

In all these ways, then, and in more which we have only implied, baptism is an obstetrical event. The church stands nearby as midwife to deliver what the Father has given life to. The danger in that imagery is that it may make us think too exclusively of infant baptism, whereas everybody's baptism is birth. It is important to keep clearly and constantly in mind that "every person . . . is an infant in Christ when he is baptized." [8] More will be said about this in the following chapter. But even here we must emphasize that, on any con-

[8] H. G. Hardin, J. D. Quillian, Jr., and J. F. White, *The Celebration of the Gospel* (Nashville: Abingdon Press, 1964), p. 114.

ceivable absolute scale, the spiritual road ahead for the adult Christian is quite as long and just as rocky as that of the baptized child. Indeed, if what Jesus said about childlikeness and Kingdom credentials is any test, that road may be lengthier and more perilous for the adult, so much has he to unlearn, lay aside, or be freed from. From the mountaintop of Switzerland's *Jungfrau* a boulder and a basketball appear pretty much of the same size. Just so, the birth of baptism requires and insures that everybody must begin at the beginning. And one man's beginning is really not that much different from another's.

To put it in liturgical language, baptism understood as birth is our introit (our entry) into baptism understood as life. It stands at the beginning as a summons and a psalm. As the Proper of the Mass, baptism is special to or appointed for this festive day, in this case a birthday, a literally blessed event. Much follows it, some of which supersedes it, but all is meant to celebrate it. In the theme of one of Sister Corita's justly famous art shows, the church in baptism gives thanks for this "life, new life." It is only a beginning but a joyous and promising one.

Baptism as birth, then, possesses a "priority [which] is logical as well as chronological. It is the inaugurating, initiating event." [9] It is a birth issuing from a prior Birth, the one in Bethlehem in Judea in the days of Herod the King. It is the entryway into a life nourished by him who *is life*. Its songs, like the songs of any nursery, are simple, direct, honest, and joyous. And, of supreme importance, they are songs scored and scaled by him who puts a new *song* into every ready heart.

[9] Carl Michalson, "Why Methodists Baptize," *Christian Advocate* (June, 1958), p. 19.

Or, to put it in doctrinal language (drawn from another sacrament), baptism as birth is the seal of the church's confidence that in this new life *Christ is really present.* What happens in the blessed sacrament, the Eucharist, has already happened in the basic sacrament, baptism: Christ dwells therein. As he identifies himself with and takes possession of the bread and the wine, so he identifies himself with and takes possession of this ordinary, elemental human life when it is set aside for his sake. As he is present to and through the offering at the altar or table, so he is present to and through the offering at the baptistry or font. This birth is filled with hope because God is its source, its companion, and its goal.

IV

Are we not now able to see that the often acrimonious debate about the mode of baptism is quite wide of the central point? We are of course quite glad and relieved that those days are long gone when zealots were slain in their own baptistries and drowned in their own blood. What we moderns may however fail to perceive is that our gentler disputes are almost equally wide of the sacramental point: immersion versus sprinkling versus pouring versus whatever aberrant innovation somebody came up with yesterday morning.

Each method does express a certain somewhat distinctive symbolic value, as recent authors have pointed out.[10] Immersion symbolizes death to self and resurrection to the new life in Christ; sprinkling symbolizes cleansing; pouring symbolizes the outpouring and overflowing Spirit of God. Hence, *"each mode is a way of understanding the whole work of Jesus*

[10] H. G. Hardin, J. D. Quillian, Jr., and J. F. White, *The Celebration of the Gospel,* p. 112.

Christ as Savior. Therefore, each mode of baptism participates in the meaning of the other two, so it does not matter which mode is used." [11]

I confess that, for adult baptism, I prefer the vigorous shock and reminder of immersion. And I suppose that mode is less in danger of becoming stylized and routine. Moreover, there is a sharp, earthy drama and reminder in the totality of immersion. Martin E. Marty speaks of this in his helpful little book called simply *Baptism*:

> The trend through the centuries has been away from the early understanding which involved relishing, drowning in, and enjoying the water of life. The baptismal river became a pool; the pool became a well or cistern; the cistern became a barrel; the barrel became a font; the font became a bird bath; the bird bath became a bowl; the bowl became a finger bowl. If the trend continues—perhaps it is not irreverent to ask—shall we soon be experiencing the waters, the Flood, the Red Sea, the Jordan, the water of life, in the minuscule antisepsis of an aerator, an atomizer, or a humidifier? [12]

Even so, mode deals only marginally with meaning. An obstetrician might be preferable to a midwife, but, after the birth, that hardly counts as crucial.

On May 22, 1750, John Wesley wrote a letter to Gilbert Royce, a Baptist clergyman. He was concerned to protect the truth that Christ wills the salvation of all men, baptized or no. He wrote: "You think the mode of baptism is 'necessary to salvation'; I deny that even baptism itself is so; if it were, every Quaker must be damned, which I can in no wise

[11] *Ibid.*, p. 112.
[12] *Baptism*, p. 16.

44

believe. I hold nothing to be (strictly speaking) necessary to salvation but the mind which was in Christ." Wesley could not casually excuse anybody for lightly dismissing what Jesus seriously enjoined. Nevertheless what Jesus enjoined was not a method, however venerable or useful or instructive. With that, perhaps, we can let the matter rest.

V

It remains now, in this chapter, to consider the relationship between baptism and confirmation.

The word "confirmation" itself appears to have occurred first in an ecclesiastical context in the fifth century (around 441) and again in a letter of Pope Leo I in 458.[13] From the very beginning (whenever that was!) the practice and its intended significance have been widely and variously disputed.

Out of all this it is difficult to form a clear picture, but its general outlines, however blurred, appear something like this: In the early church, when a person repented his sins and publicly declared his sincere resolve to follow Christ The Way, he was baptized, probably by immersion, in the presence of other previously committed followers of The Way. He then became a special concern of the Wayfaring Church. To his nurture during this "nursery" period they devoted particular attention. He was suckled on the facts about Jesus —instruction—and spoon-fed on the celebration of these facts—worship (holy communion excepted). When he had reached the toddler stage, ready to try to walk on his own though still with the helping hand of the church on his, he

[13] See D. M. Baillie, *The Theology of the Sacraments,* p. 90 n.

was given an opportunity to "confirm" the vows he had earlier taken or, in some cases, the vows taken for him.

Confirmation thus was the other side of the coin of baptism or, to employ our present analogy, the exit from the nursery. So at least has a considerable corpus of Christian thought customarily understood confirmation: not as an act which tends to subtract from baptism but as a consequent affirmation which extends the effects of baptism throughout life. Bishop Robinson speaks for a host of often otherwise widely divergent churchmen when he says, "Confirmation . . . essentially is the last act of the baptismal liturgy, rather than a second, or superior, rite. The theological emphasis is laid on the Baptism, of which Confirmation is the crown . . . rather than on Confirmation, of which Baptism is the preliminary." [14]

This seems to us the probable, and anyway an understandable, interpretation of the twin though conjoined practices of baptism and confirmation.

It opens numerous possibilities. Among them is the thoroughly ancient, thoroughly modern, thoroughly endurable conviction that in confirmation one joins the world quite as much as he does the church.

Once more, however, a warning, again from the pen of Marty who rightly observes,

> Confirmation is ill-defined in the Protestant tradition. Perhaps this is fortunate. It is a salutary rite of the church because it provides the opportunity for instruction and the undertaking of personal resolves. But most attempts to define it too precisely as a ratification of baptism, a personal reasserting of baptismal vows to "make them mind," issue in a failure to pre-

[14] John A. T. Robinson, *Liturgy Coming to Life* (Philadelphia: Westminster Press, 1964), p. 40.

serve the uniqueness of the baptismal promise. They imply an incompleteness about baptism to which the New Testament does not admit.[15]

That in very large part is our point: Baptism is complete, as a birth is. It is an event followed by a process. Father Fiedler will come to terms with the process in the next chapter.

[15] *Baptism,* p. 43.

[4]

BAPTISM AS LIFE

Whatever may be the developments in the evolution of practices pro and con infant baptism, the subject can serve as a convenient introduction to this discussion of "Baptism as Life."

We have already considered baptism as birth. However, simply being born is never enough. For one thing, it does not necessarily mean being accepted. Today we are at least somewhat aware of the tragedies that occur whenever there exists a case of an unwanted child. And we are also somewhat aware that birth into such a family is usually the beginning of a scarred life, filled with suffering because of the serious psychological problems engendered from the lack of love. In order to truly live fully, the newborn must be received, be accepted by his parents, the first human community, with love. Psychology and medicine have told the world in irrefutable terms that this love must be there, and clearly expressed, from birth. Even the first days, months, and years are crucial, notwithstanding the fact that the newborn does not at that period *know* this. Infant baptism, if it served no other

48

purpose, is a clear sign from the larger community, the church, that this newborn *is accepted* by the larger church community, and accepted with love at any time, any age that he is born into it. That the church has been conscious of this is evident even in some denominations that have not recently made a practice of celebrating baptism as a community event. Let us keep firmly in mind that this is not merely a sociological grouping but the dynamic presence of Christ in his people.

To continue with the concept of new human life: Having been conceived, born, and received in life with love, life itself still follows. The need to grow and develop in the community that conceived, bore, and accepted the individual continues unabated.

This is equally true of the newly baptized and remains so for his growth into the mature Christian, and throughout his Christian life.

Perhaps increased attention to this communal aspect of the sacrament of baptism would indicate areas of possible ecumenical development as the churches move into greater unity once more.

It is not digressing, I believe, to observe that the rite itself deserves a great deal of attention. Accretions of many centuries deposited in the baptismal rituals are not all equally felicitous additions. At the present, some of these additions to ritual seem to obscure the simplicity of the baptismal sign rather than clarify it. In some of the rituals, the community aspect is virtually crowded out of practical existence. We should also be concerned to study and develop this from an ecumenical stance. Such study is particularly timely since the major Christian denominations have now gone on record publicly, recognizing the validity of one another's baptism as incorporation into Christ. And with the public recognition of validity of one another's baptism on the part of the various Christian denominations, we have, besides our common humanity, the most solid and profound foundation of the ecumenical movement. To illustrate the Roman Catholic position, the Vatican Council stated, "By the sacrament of baptism, whenever it is properly conferred in the way the Lord determined, and received with the appropriate dispositions of soul, a man becomes truly incorporated into the crucified and glorified Christ and is reborn to a sharing of the divine life, as the apostle says: 'For you were buried together with him in Baptism, and in him also rose again through faith in the working of God who raised him from the dead.' " (Col. 2: 12; cf. Rom. 6:4) [1]

> Baptism, therefore, constitutes a sacramental bond of unity linking all who have been reborn by means of it. But baptism, of itself, is only a beginning, a point of departure, for it is wholly directed toward the acquiring of fullness of life in Christ. Baptism is thus oriented toward a complete . . . participation in Eucharistic communion.[2]

Vatican Council II further states:

> The Catholic Church accepts them [i.e. separated brothers] with respect and affection as brothers. . . . Undoubtedly, the differences that exist in varying degrees between them and the Catholic Church—whether in doctrine and sometimes in discipline, or concerning the structure of the Church—do indeed create many and sometimes serious obstacles to full ecclesiastical communion. These the ecumenical movement is striving to overcome. Nevertheless, all those justified by faith through

---

[1] *The Documents of Vatican II,* "Ecumenism," No. 22, pp. 363-64.
[2] *Ibid.,* "Ecumenism," No. 22, p. 364.

baptism are incorporated into Christ. They therefore have a right to be honored by the title of Christian, and are properly regarded as brothers in the Lord by the sons of the Catholic Church.

Moreover some, even very many, of the most significant elements or endowments which together go to build up and give life to the Church herself can exist outside the visible boundaries of the Catholic Church; the written word of God; the life of grace; faith, hope, and charity, along with other interior gifts of the Holy Spirit and visible elements. All of these, which come from Christ and lead back to Him, belong by right to the one Church of Christ.[3]

As a Roman Catholic, I am particularly happy to call attention to this statement.

The communal aspect of baptism requires us to say that it is not only individual birth into the person of Christ but the birth of the individual into the communal body of Christ as a new living member! But must we not say this more clearly?

Baptism is the beginning of a new way of life. One becomes "a new man" in Christ. We "put on Christ" and begin the process of "growing up to full maturity" in him, in his life of service, of giving, his life of love of the Father, mankind, and the world.

This life will be reflected in the increasing impetus to be of service for others. The dimension of unselfishness in this service should be increasingly evident as the individual grows in his own maturing love of and within the community. Generosity in sensing and responding to the needs of others,

[3] *Ibid.*, "Ecumenism," No. 3, pp. 345-46.

51

even if at a cost of personal inconvenience or difficulty, becomes a distinguishing mark of the truly living Christian.

In short, without endangering individuality, the essential lines of Christ's own life become constantly more evident in both the Christian individual and the community, as they attempt to further the incarnational process by extending Christ to the contemporary world. This is true not only of social action but of prayer and worship as well. It must permeate all of life.

The Vatican II Council states:

The Church must be present in these groups of men through those of her children who dwell among them or are sent to them. For wherever they live, all Christians are bound to show forth, by the example of their lives and by the witness of their speech, that new man which they put on at baptism, and that power of the Holy Spirit by whom they were strengthened at confirmation. Thus other men, observing their good works, can glorify the Father (cf. Mt. 5:16) and can better perceive the real meaning of human life and the bond which ties the whole community of mankind together.

That they may be able to give this witness to Christ fruitfully, let them be joined to those men by esteem and love, and acknowledge themselves to be members of the group of men among whom they live. Let them share in cultural and social life by the various exchanges and enterprises of human living. Let them be familiar with their national and religious traditions, gladly and reverently laying bare the seeds of the Word which lie hidden in them.

All the members ought to be modelled on him, until Christ be formed in them. For this reason we, who have been made to conform with him, who have died with him and risen with

52

him, are taken up into the mysteries of his life, until we will reign together with him. While still pilgrims on earth, tracing in trial and in oppression the paths he trod, we are associated with his sufferings as the body is with the head, suffering with him, that with him we may be glorified.[4]

In truth, however, not only baptism but all sacraments, all worship are cast in the dimension of a community. The signs and symbols of the sacraments must not unite an individual with the redemptive event of Christ only, but they must unite him also with his neighbor in the believing community, with the church itself. In sacraments, individuals do not encounter Christ alone, they encounter him in the living, believing community.

The Lord is always revealing himself to the world with new and fresh insights. We should anticipate discovering these possibilities in the social and cultural areas of concern contemporary with our own life-span. It is in this way, in accepting Christian baptism as beginning a way of life, that the incarnation is made present and effective through all the years that will pass between the Lord's physical disappearance and his return. The ecumenical development of this age is the clearest evidence of this continuing presence for us today. As we recognize this and begin to be increasingly modified in our own Christian behavior by it, we must begin increased efforts so to state our faith in the practices and disciplines of our churches. For example, at the Valparaiso Liturgical Institute in 1968, the Reverend H. Boone Porter, Jr., professor of liturgics at the General Theological seminary, New York, an Episcopalian, made some interesting suggestions about ecumenical norms for the baptismal liturgy.

[4] *Ibid.*, "Missions," No. 11, pp. 597-9; "The Church," No. 7, p. 21.

He first considers the *time* of baptism. Promiscuous and indiscriminate baptism has little to recommend it, outside danger of death, even though it is not difficult to see historical reasons that encouraged this rather general practice. Easter, with the Resurrection festivities, is the most appropriate of times for "rising to new life in Christ." However, Pentecost and the intervening fifty days are also appropriate. So also would be the feast of the commemoration of our Lord's baptism at Epiphany time, the feast of all Saints in the fall, the patronal feast of the parish or its anniversary. To emphasize such times as normative is to permit the possibility of greater community involvement in a more meaningful, developed rite that can be a true celebration.

Professor Porter invisions a delay of baptism generally until an age when a person can make some commitment of his own—a possibility that is even being considered by some Roman Catholic theologians today (I will not remark on their popularity). In view of what has been said here in the previous chapter, however, both authors of this book opt for infant baptism.

Turning his attention to the *procedure* of baptism, Professor Porter sees several significant phases or actions:

First, there should be pre-baptismal instruction. The entire process should begin with a prayer and blessing to mark the entrance on the road leading to baptism. Next, he recommends a greater selectivity in the choice of scripture readings, to be followed by a homily, hymns between the readings, hallowing of the water, affirmation of the Christian faith, and the baptism itself with the customary formula. These would not present insurmountable pastoral problems if, as suggested above, baptism were normally restricted to certain times.

54

In Porter's opinion, the only way to discuss ecumenically the use of the water is to discuss getting people wet—really wet.

Then he adds one of his ecumenically most interesting recommendations. He urges first that confirmation follow baptism immediately. I realize that consensus on the meaning of what the churches variously call "confirmation" is only at a genesis stage of understanding. But let us pass that for the moment. This is not an impossible consideration even for Roman Catholics, in view of the more extended facilities for pastors to confirm in danger of death, the greater use of deans or vicar-generals as ministers, etc. He also urges a restoration of the practice of uniting "first communion" with what would become an overall rite of Christian initiation. This, too, is not without precedent in our churches' heritage.

Baptismal life comes truly and fully alive in the Eucharist. The eucharistic liturgy at such times could then simply begin with the offering of gifts, the foregoing taking the place of the Service of the Word. This arrangement would permit the entire congregation to join the new members at the altar, and the reality of birth and growth in Christ in the community would become more evident.

These are interesting suggestions. We must, in all efforts to make sacraments more meaningful, which is to say to allow Christ to be more accessible, strive always to be simple. His words and gestures in Palestine were supremely simple instruments of communication. What we call baptism is as basic and simple as birth. It can be traumatic or easy and will remain always one of the great human mysteries. But we do not commonly clutter it. We have no need to. It speaks for itself. Let us keep baptism simple and accessible. In this way, perhaps, we can assist the continuation and maturing of that new life as a more conscious and believable meeting with him. Let us try to keep encountering him—him into whom we have been born anew without trappings or subterfuge.

"For me to live is Christ." Baptism sets us in this dimension; life itself, daily growing in him achieves it.

[5]

EUCHARIST, I

The lean and unimaginative titles we have given to this
and the next chapter are a reverse tribute to the rich and
inexhaustible meaning of what nearly all Christians would
be content to call simply *the* sacrament. Anyway, they would
understand which sacrament was being designated by this un-
adorned term. *The* sacrament, in history, in doctrine, and in
personal experience, can refer to none other than the one
instituted when Jesus broke the bread, blessed the cup, and
commanded his men to do likewise through all the ages.

No single title seems to do justice to this singular sacrament. Various ages in the church's history and various stages
of her doctrine have emphasized one or another aspect of
the sacrament. The very multiplicity of its titles testifies to
this: Lord's Supper, Last Supper, Holy Communion, Mass,
Blessed Sacrament, Eucharist.

We have selected Eucharist because it seems to us to
impart the tone and describe the content of all of these. This
sacrament, in each of its parts and in totality, is an act of
thanksgiving.

I

The very word "Eucharist" means just that, in both its
linguistic roots and its liturgical usage. As to the former, its

parent and grandparent words in Latin and Greek mean "to show favor" or "to give thanks." As to the latter, the sacramental liturgies are redolent with the fragrance of *thanksgiving.*

Consider: Almost at the outset, "We give thanks . . . for thy great glory. . . ." At the offertory we are summoned to "offer unto God thanksgiving; and pay . . . vows unto the most High." Before the Prayer of Consecration we lift the ancient hymn, "Let us give thanks unto the Lord . . . ; it is very meet, right, and our bounden duty that we should at all times and in all places give thanks unto thee, O Lord. . . ." In the midst and at the heart of the consecration itself we are reminded that, "when he had given thanks, he brake it, and . . . he took the cup; and when he had given thanks, he gave it to them. . . ." When we make our communion, it is accompanied by the cadence of the glad command, "Feed on Him in your heart by faith, with thanksgiving. . . . Drink this . . . and be thankful." In the Prayer of Thanksgiving itself, of course, we humbly beseech God to "accept this our sacrifice of praise and thanksgiving." The sacrament is saturated with thanksgiving; the liturgy lives in its light.

More basically we begin this consideration of the Holy Meal with the element of thanksgiving because the human family does. People observe all kinds of occasions by eating together: wedding anniversaries, birthdays, retirement parties, reunions, even (in the countryside at least) funerals. These vital milestones are made memorable by the breaking of bread, the lifting of cups, and, among the religious, the making of prayers. The element of thanksgiving usually is not altogether absent even when men eat bread in sadness. They remember, with thankfulness, the virtues and strengths of a departed loved one or the accomplishment and ideals of a defeated homeland. On other occasions, on the last Thursday in November, for example, the element of thanksgiving is not simply the seasoning: It is the feast.

One fears that this symbolic, spiritual, value-laden aspect of the common meal is being lost in many homes (even, I gently remind my co-author, in many priestly celibate homes). Meals are for mastication, not celebration, and not much even of that. This is the age of the dietary prefix and the culinary afterthought. If it is not pre-cooked, it is pre-frozen, pre-baked or pre-seasoned—anyway, preprepared. The only thing these non-meals are not is pre-digested, and to the development of even that, no doubt, some bright young marketing expert on the make is probably devoting his every waking hour. This is the age of the automat, the TV dinner, the synthetic flavoring or coloring, the houses without dining rooms, and the families without dinner hours. About the only place we dine anymore is six miles up in the sky, and even then we are in such a hurry that we eat our appetizer high over Cleveland and gulp our dessert barely over New York. Even so, over much of the world and over most of history sensitive persons have understood that the meal is a meaningful event, not a necessary nuisance. The appropriation of the sacrament as Eucharist requires the recovery of that understanding.

We begin with thanksgiving also because the early church did. The very oldest part of our extant liturgy is the *Sursum Corda*, an almost reckless hymn of joy. "Lift up your hearts," said the priest or presbyter, very probably almost shouting. To which the people responded, with equal abandon. "We lift them unto the Lord." The whole affair had a rollicking beat to it which, if it were reproduced in the average present-day parish church, would shake the faithful to their mani-

59

cured fingertips—and strike them as sacrilegious to boot. Yet this was the tone and content of the earliest celebrations: "Let us make Eucharist unto our God!"

We have chosen to commence with thanksgiving also because Christian experience does. The note of joy, the tone of gladness, was not something either imposed on the sacrament or peculiar to it. It arose out of the life and grew from the gospel of which the sacrament was but a single though supreme part. I suppose to those outside the living room of the church it seemed a sort of ritualist charade, but no one inside had to guess its meaning! It was a grateful dramatization of the great fact that "God was in Christ, reconciling the world unto himself"—reconciling even that part of the world which had not yet deciphered the charade. It was an acted sermon based upon the text, "Thanks be to God who gives us the victory through Jesus Christ." It was the liturgical celebration of the life which was always serious but seldom somber and never in despair. Thus it was a profound insight when John Wesley, adapting the Book of Common Prayer for the use of the people called Methodist in America, dropped from the General Confession of Sins the phrase, "the burthen of them is intolerable." Since Christ—let us give Eucharist—that is simply not true. They are burdensome, but One bears them with us, so they are not intolerable. The pedagogy of the human heart, if it has itself been instructed by Christ, teaches man that his natal word is "thanksgiving."

The Protestant traditions, it seems to this particular Protestant, have a rather splotchy record of giving thanks. It is probable that the popular image of the Puritan as unrelievedly dour and humorously joyless is stereotypical. So diverse and independent a lot were they that almost any generalization about them would be false. Nevertheless, this notion doubtless has some anchor in fact, even if it is anchored in the backwaters of a stagnating and fetid puritanism. One is reminded of the wry remark of the Scottish "dominie" after hearing the people at the kirk lumber their way through the singing of a psalm. "If this be their joy," he exclaimed, "what can be their lamentation"—(an observation, one adds, which need not be limited to Scots or to Puritans or to an earlier century)! That is precisely my present point. Far too much of this severe religion, which mistakes austerity for awe and simplicity for celebration, has spilled over into our own. It has contributed to what might be called the cold shower concept of Christianity: in order for something to be religiously valid, so the often unspoken argument goes, it has to elicit from us a kind of theological "brrrr." If it is fun, it is wrong; if it is beautiful, it is bad; if it is pleasant, it is "unspiritual," whatever that means. Protestant Christianity has not ever exhausted nor always expressed its chartered gladness. This is odd, for ours is a faith (or so we say) with grace at the head of it and therefore (one would suppose) with joy at the heart of it.

Nor has the Roman Catholic expression always done a great deal better. Much of the music of her Mass as well as the paucity of her hymnody and the feebleness of her candlelight suggests just about everything except glad and lifted hearts. Even the gossipy garrulousness of Protestants in the pews would sometimes be a welcome relief from the mumbled lethargy of Catholics at their prayers.

The reason for these dolorous devotions, on both sides of the Reformation wall, is the concentration of Western religion on the atonement. Yet even that is a sad, and consequently saddening, misunderstanding. Properly understood the love of God never shone more brightly forth than on Good Friday. Its liturgical colors should be the white of hope (as Rome has recently recognized) or even the red of celebration. Anyway, for whatever reason, we are both collectively guilty of draping too much of the gospel in black.

Perhaps we should take a hint from our Eastern Orthodox brethren who have understood more fully than have we that really the gospel both opens and climaxes with "good tidings of great joy, which shall be to all people" (Luke 2:10). The text of all worship, if it is genuinely eucharistic, should be "thanks to God who gives us the victory through Jesus Christ." Romano Guardini has a famous chapter bearing the delightful title, "The Playfulness of the Liturgy." Let us then in the name of God make bold to play, with thankful hearts. To that we are urgently summoned in the sacrament of thanksgiving.

II

Secondly, the Eucharist is the sacrament of *presence*.

The doctrine of the real presence of Christ in the sacrament has undergone considerable development, not necessarily to say distortion, in the course of the centuries. In the early centuries, the church was content mostly to proclaim the presence, wisely spending little energy in speculating upon the *how* of it. Both Ambrose and Augustine spoke of Christ's being in the bread but implied no metaphysical change therein. John of Damascus, writing four centuries later, did refer to "change" in the communion elements but does not spell out his meaning.

A century later still, a treatise was published entitled, *De corpore et sanguine domini* (*The Lord's Body and Blood*), authored by Paschasius Radbertus, the abbot of Corbie. It was a historical and pioneering book, the first ever published devoted exclusively to the Eucharist.[1] Abbot Radbertus asserted that at the consecration the bread and the wine became identified with the natural body of Christ. Radbertus immediately found himself in a theological squabble with Ratramnus, a monk of Corbie. The latter undertook to disprove his superior's position in most vigorous terms. By that time, clearly nothing resembling consensus had been achieved. However, by the eleventh century the view espoused by Radbertus stood at the top of the theological Gallup polls.[2]

The Reformers for their part (except Zwinglians) argued against the how of the presence but not against the faith-filled fact of it. One customary way of putting it was that Christ was present in the *total* sacramental act, not exclusively in the bread and the wine. (Subsequently some of the disciples and interpreters of the Reformers reintroduced the original problem with their own formulas and with new disputes about the how, like consubstantiation.) Even that strong and stubborn Scot, Robert Bruce, who was born just before the Reformation but who was to be its chief stabilizer in his homeland, was able to say (speaking of the elements or species) in St. Giles,' Edinburgh: "I call them signs because they have the Body and Blood of Christ conjoined to them . . . ; if they did nothing but represent or signify a thing absent, then any picture or dead image would be a sacrament." [3]

We can conclude, therefore, that Stephen F. Winward

---

[1] See G. E. McCracken and Allen Cabaniss, eds., *Early Medieval Theology,* "The Library of Christian Classics," IX (Philadelphia: Westminster Press, 1957), 91.

[2] Kenneth G. Phifer, *A Protestant Case for Liturgical Renewal* (Philadelphia: Westminster Press, 1965), pp. 42-43.

[3] *The Mystery of the Lord's Supper* (London: J. Clarke, 1958), p. 44.

in his excellent study, *The Reformation of Our Worship,* speaks for a whole cloud of sacramental witnesses—primitive, medieval, Reformation, and modern—when he says that "Eucharist is encounter because Christ is present." [4] As we shall see in Father Fiedler's chapter on the Eucharist, this is a judgment remarkably similar to that of Professor Schillebeeckx in his pivotal volume, *Christ the Sacrament of the Encounter with God.*

Perhaps a Methodist may observe that our tradition, stemming as it does from the same Catholic sources by way of the Church of England, is entirely consonant with this. Most of our eucharistic doctrine, appropriately, is embedded in song. Consider the most meager of samplings, drawn almost at random from *The Eucharistic Hymns of John and Charles Wesley:*

> In the Rite Thou hast enjoin'd
> Let us now our Savior find.

> Give what these Hallo'd Signs express . . .
> The Sign transmits the Signified.

> We come with Confidence to find
> Thy special Presence here . . .
> His Presence makes the Feast.

Then, supremely, this:

> We need not now go up to Heaven
> To bring the long-sought Savior down;
> Thou art to all already given,

[4] *The Reformation of Our Worship* (Richmond, Va.: John Knox Press, 1965), p. 27.

> Thou dost even now Thy banquet crown:
> To every faithful soul appear
> And show Thy real presence here! [5]

Wesley (either Wesley) refuses futile speculation on the manner of the presence, but he also refuses to compromise on the reality of it. In one of his letters, John Wesley writes, concerning what he calls "the Holy Sacrament": "His divinity is so united to us then . . . , though the manner of that union is utterly a mystery to me." [6] As one of the "stewards of the mysteries of God" (I Cor. 4:1) he was obligated to say no less and able to say no more.

It is true that Wesley occasionally betrays an inadequate understanding of what he sometimes calls "Romish doctrine," as for example in the hymnic polemic against a "local diety." [7] He apparently "did not know that the doctrine of transubstantiation specifically excludes the confinement of God to place." [8] Nevertheless, as one Roman Catholic scholar judges, "A great majority of Charles's hymns on the Eucharist could be sung in a Catholic Church." [9] Increasingly, they are even sung in Methodist churches! Anyway, wherever sung, they very much coincide with the consensus of a great deal of church doctrine.

We must admit that Protestantism has within it a strong minority voice which prevents this song of sacramental ecumenicity from being sung in unison or without discord. I refer to the "memorialist" or Zwinglian alternative. Indeed I

[5] John Ernest Rattenbury, *The Eucharistic Hymns of John and Charles Wesley* (London: Epworth Press, 1948), Nos. 33, 47, 81, 116.

[6] *Letters* (London: Epworth Press, 1931), I, 118.

[7] *The Eucharistic Hymns of John and Charles Wesley*, no. 63.

[8] John M. Todd, *John Wesley and the Catholic Church* (London, Hodder & Stroughton, 1952), p. 148.

[9] *Ibid.*

65

strongly suspect that, if one were to scratch the ecclesiastical epidermis of the average unreflective Protestant, what one would find beneath the surface would be an irritated Zwinglian.

I would protest, however, that this residual Zwinglianism is caused by a misunderstanding of what must be the most seriously undertranslated word in sacramental history, namely the Greek word *anamnesis,* usually translated as "remembrance" or "memorial." Dom Gregory Dix in his monumental study, *The Shape of the Liturgy,* points out that these words have "for us a connotation of something itself absent. . . . But in the scriptures . . . [the cognate verbs] have the sense of 're-calling' or 're-presenting' before God an event, . . . so that it becomes *here and now* operative by its effect." [10] The biblically more adequate understanding of "remembrance," however, is that it is a prelude to presence.

Eugene Stockwell relates an event which takes place in communist China and which vividly illustrates the way remembrance reaches livingly into the present.

> In a banquet a Christian who dared not be overt in his faith took a piece of bread and unobtrusively but significantly broke it, and as he did, he said, "I remember." A few others round the table who noticed this quietly ate bread also. Moments later the same man took a glass of water and, prior to taking a sip, again said, "I remember." Others did likewise. . . . The sacrament of Holy Communion had been reenacted, the Christian community was present, the hope was kept alive.[11]

To be sure, a sturdy root of mystery grows beneath this presence of Christ, as it does beneath all worship or, for that

[10] *The Shape of the Liturgy* (Naperville, Ill.: Allenson, 2nd ed., 1945).
[11] *Claimed by God for Mission* (New York: World Outlook Press, 1965), p. 132.

matter, beneath most that men call real, under whatever rubric. If we uproot the mystery, what we get is not simply a shriveled sacrament or a moribund gospel. Both sacrament and gospel live in the soil of mystery. It is mysterious that an unauthorized rabbi should stand in for God. It is mysterious that one who came to death on a criminal's gibbet should be named the Lord of Life. Charles Wesley sings, shifting the metaphor, "Veiled in flesh, the godhead see"; but that veil of mystery hung over the entire enterprise from the beginning and always will.

Yet, speaking personally, this veil of mystery is forever preferable to that nude rationalism which tries to tear away the veil but succeeds only in getting enwrapped in it. It knows neither song nor poetry, neither rhapsody nor awe. In its aim to explain the whole, it leaves us only with a knotted, tattered, and shredded part. And—not the least of its penalties—it cannot even despair with wholeheartedness, so busy is it describing the knots, the shreds, and the parts.

Furthermore, Christ is present in his sacrament *because* he is already present in his world and through his people. If you care or dare to uproot *that*, the alternative is starkly this: If this is not the sacrament of the real presence, then it is the sacrament of the real absence. Gordon Rupp recalls "seeing a conservative evangelical Anglican college in Australia where over the communion table were the words, 'He is not here!' " [12] That would make us of all men most forlorn.

III

Third, the Eucharist is a sacrament of *sacrifice*. Here we confront our greatest difficulties. No Protestant could possibly

[12] Dow Kirkpatrick, ed. *The Finality of Christ* (Nashville: Abingdon Press, 1966), p. 180.

mean by "sacrifice" what the Council of Trent seems to make it mean for Roman Catholics (although that latter Communion is in such rapid transition and reassessment that we shall expect Father Fiedler to say precisely what bearing Trent has on contemporary Catholicism). Still, whether we are considering the blunt words of Bishop Andrew de Cuesta of León in a debate at Trent: "Christ in a way dies and is slain by the priest," or Pope John XXIII's weighty sentence in *Ad Petri Cathedram*, "In this Sacrifice Christ himself . . . is daily immolated for us all, as once on Calvary when hanging on the cross"—the theological barriers for the Protestant are, if not insurmountable, at least higher than he can presently reach. I phrase it thus frankly because the purpose of an ecumenical dialogue is not to obscure difficulties, not to imagine differences out of existence, and also because Father Fiedler will have an opportunity in the following chapter to make answer.

Anyway, however far from the New Testament such statements seem, and whatever the New Testament *does* mean when it speaks of sacrifice, what is undeniable is that the sacrificial element has been explicitly recorded in the Eucharist from the time of the Didache onward. Moreover, it does have, or can have, a meaning from the Protestant perspective, and I now turn to its explication.

Part of the difficulty may well be that Medieval thinkers and Reformers alike were not entirely biblical in their dominant ideas of sacrifice. In the Old Testament, "the death of the victim was not the end of the sacrifice, but the necessary means to the release and offering of his life." [13]

[13] I regret that I am unable to identify my literary indebtedness in the above phrase. The Reformers were right in their judgment that the sacrifice of Christ need not and cannot be repeated, wrong in their easy

John Wesley, for his part, gave the following judgment: "We believe there is, and always was, in every Christian church (whether dependent on the Bishop of Rome or not), . . . an outward sacrifice offered therein by men authorized to act as pastors of Christ and stewards of the mysteries of God." [14] He never, however, defines exactly what he means by such an "outward sacrifice" except to indicate that is was corporate. The inference is "that the Church collectively offering herself to God in the Eucharist is actually offering to God the Body of Christ—for the Church is His Body." [15] And Charles, forever setting John's logic to music, lined out the call to "restore the daily sacrifice." [16]

It is manifestly difficult to do simultaneous justice to both the logical case and the lyrical case for sacrifice. To come down too hard or too exclusively upon the logical is to sound too much like Trent. To concentrate too singly upon the lyrical is to put beauty above truth and thus to do violence to both. Modern Christians, it seems to me, are obligated resolutely to live in the tension between the two. Sacrifice is a very nearly universal characteristic of religion. Why it is, is difficult to state. That it is, is impossible to ignore. What it accomplishes or how, we do not and apparently cannot precisely know. What we do know is that in the presence of the necessity or of the exemplars of sacrifice, men have sacrificed, pouring out their best thought and singing their

---

equation of his sacrifice with his death. The sacrifice of Christ was his total life, including his death but not limited to it. Had this been understood by both sides and had the language and its nuances been tuned in on communication rather than been polemic, a great deal of grief might have been averted.

[14] *Letters*, II, 58.

[15] John Ernest Rattenbury, *The Eucharistic Hymns of John and Charles Wesley*, p. 132.

[16] *Ibid.*, No. 166, stanza 16.

sweetest songs in the effort to make it clear and compelling. Perhaps we should never have tried to say more than that —a possibility Catholics might ponder. But certainly we should never have avoided saying less than that, a fact which Protestants might ponder.

Ponder and pursue—which, at the very least, leads us straightway to the certain knowledge that the eucharistic sacrifice involves and requires the sacrifice of ourselves and our substance, "of our souls and bodies" as the prayer of thanksgiving puts it. "Do this in remembrance" means, *"All of you do this breaking and pouring out with your lives."* Behind the consecrated elements stand consecrated men and women:

> Thou dost give Thyself to me,
> May I give myself to Thee.[17]

IV

Finally, the Eucharist is a sacrament of *unity*. We may just be on the verge of the most important ecumenical breakthrough, doctrinely speaking, since the Reformation. Gregory Baum has recently written of what he takes to be an inescapable implication of Vatican II. That is, the affirmation "that Baptism creates a unity in Christ which no subsequent division among Christians can undo." [18]

The implications of this are simply staggering or will be if they are followed up with sympathy and vigor. For example, if what constitutes a person a Christian is baptism, that uni-

---

[17] Cf. the 7th stanza of "On this day, the first of days"; Latin (Carcassonne Breviary 1745), trans. H. W. Baker.
[18] "Liturgy and Unity," *Ecumenist*, V (November-December, 1967), 99.

versal ordination to the universal priesthood, then marriages between Christians, even of different churches, are valid. If baptism is the mark and measure for unity, then our eucharistic separateness may turn out to be the starkest kind of theological inconsistency. Such inconsistency amounts to our saying—with doctrinally straight faces yet—"We are already and indissolubly one in Christ our common Lord. We are his family. This is his Table. He is our bread. Nevertheless, we will stay at separate Tables because—well, because we have for four hundred and fifty years." Which is to say, we are guilty not only of stark inconsistency but of impious disobedience.

Surely not! Yet—we may as well confess it—until we are ready to say "surely not!" with ready resolution, what should be the crown of our unity is instead, again, a crown of thorns. Until we are ready reverently to act upon *that,* then the bread which is broken, while it remains a token of our self-giving Lord, is a token, too, of his self-divided people. The very common elements of our Holy Communion—grain, gathered and ground and baked into bread; grapes, crushed and blended into wine—remind us that, until we are one, Christ is divided.[19]

It might help if once in a while we commissioned a New Testament scholar to celebrate the sacrament so that he could remind us that the command of the Lord, "This do . . . ," is geared to a plural verb. The Eucharist is not a private compact or a personal devotion. It is a corporate command: "This you all do, together. Or else [might he not add?] it is not fully done."

[19] We are already one, of course. Our unity is not something produced by us but given to us in Christ. But the practical problem of expressing this given fact remains.

This brings us right back to where this chapter started, to the meals by which men mark their gladness and their tears. Jesus, remember, marked the fact of community by the act of breaking bread. Included in that community were sinners. So he ate with sinners. It was just that simple, profound, stringent, merciful—and imperative.

I conclude this chapter with a parable, though an actual happening in Cuba. Eugene Stockwell tells the story:

A large Havana Church . . . holds informal weekly home meetings in various sections of the city. I asked if I might attend one and was cordially welcomed. About twenty of us crowded into the home of a . . . layman, while two armed militiamen stood at the door. . . . This layman had faced the death of his wife only weeks before. I expected this would be a home shrouded in tragedy but found it to be a place of serene . . . Christian faith and joy. Gathered there . . . were some who were quite favorable to Fidel Castro's revolution and others deeply opposed to it. The meeting began with conversation about the topics of most interest to the group—food rationing, a child who would be operated on the next day, the problems some faced in their daily jobs. A young minister's wife played an accordion, and we sang some favorite hymns. There was a period of prayer, and finally all was gathered up into a simple yet deeply moving communion service. The same . . . elements were passed out to Cubans and to a U. S. citizen, to defenders and opponents of Fidel Castro, to Negroes and whites, to children and adults. In that moment we were one in Christ.[20]

Thanksgiving, presence, sacrifice, and *unity.* These are the sacrament of the Eucharist. God speed the day!

[20] *Claimed by God for Mission,* pp. 31-32.

[6]

EUCHARIST, II

To do what the Lord did.

Again we are concerned with the use of very simple, fundamental elements, as simple and accessible as was Jesus' own appearance and presence in Palestine.

Perhaps we can begin unraveling some of the mystery of the Eucharist by trying to find, as best we can, exactly what simple action he performed. Ecumenically, part of the present inaccessibility of the meaning of Christ (and of the Eucharist) to ecumenical efforts is the result of the mysterious clothing in which we have wrapped him, rather than the result of eucharistic mystery itself.

What did he do? What did he want to signify?

He wished to nourish us, to make us one with himself, to make us one with one another. He wished to make his sacrifice of himself present to us "until he comes." He wished to give thanks to the Father.

Therefore he took bread and wine, "gave thanks," and gave them to eat. A simple action, and a basic one. The only new element in his action, and it was almost unbelievably new, was his statement that this food was his body and blood. If so, then not only physical nourishment but the possibility of startling union in some fashion with him and, in the common eating of it, with one another was his intention. Among these same startling words, he said that this was his body which would be given for us and his blood which would be shed for us. His *sacrifice* of himself is to be present also.

These are the bare facts. All else we must examine critically to determine if it is not perhaps something that man, with undoubted good faith, once used as contemporary clothing for this simple yet most profound action. Some we will find to be rather basic articles of attire that the mind of man, probing the mystery for centuries, has devised as useful; many other elements will be far less essential word clothing, sadly dated and outmoded, stiffly uncompromising like an autocratic and somewhat defiant old maid who persists in wearing the outmoded wardrobe of an age long past. In such a situation, the language and attire of the individual may be able to reflect the true personal being of the individual *to* that individual. They may even express it adequately enough, but only to that individual. It does not encourage a more general dialogue with others.

Has such stiff costuming been true of the external language attire we have given the doctrine of the Eucharist? I think it has.

Roman Catholics have been talking about the real presence and transubstantiation of the Lord in this sacrament of love and unity for some time. They understand what they mean, we trust. But it is also evident that many Protestant Christians have looked upon the intent of this article of word clothing with some concern. For if the words are taken absolutely, without reference to the whole or to their intent, they allow an interpretation that could seem to indicate that his presence in the elements of bread and wine is understood in the most crassly material way imaginable. The recipient of communion might on occasion wonder if the Lord's head or feet entered the mouth first. Or, in that frame of reference, it would seem to indicate that if the bread were subjected to chemical analysis, one would be able to record the hemoglobin and the relative proportion of red and while blood cells.

What, surely, these words really intend to convey are simply what Jesus said and did as outlined above. There are simple and devoted Christians among these Romans Catholics, ignorant of Thomistic categories and consequently of the philosophical meaning of a word like transubstantiation. They simply believe *because he said so*. One sometimes regrets a more educated world that asks more.

It is not that Roman Catholic doctrine has indicated this confusion, but some extraordinary narrations of piety have perhaps been assumed to be doctrinal statements, and no one cried, "Wait!" Let us say once and for all that there is a vast difference between doctrine which intends to be objective, and piety which, even though it may be doctrinally based, is inevitably subjective.

The first is necessary and the other inevitable, but one still could wish that both could translate themselves to the normal Christian more simply. All sacraments are, after all, ways of touching *him*—and of him to touch us. They fulfill a need something like Thomas' need to touch him on the very night of the Resurrection. And like John's words in his

75

first letter quoted earlier, which merit some repetition in this reference:

> We write to you about the Word of life, which has existed from the beginning: We have *heard* it, and we have *seen* it with our eyes; yes we have *seen* it, and out hands have *touched* it. When this life became *visible,* we saw it; so we speak of it and tell you about the eternal life which was with the Father and was made known to us!

> What we have seen and heard we tell to you also, so that you will join with us in the fellowship that we have with the Father and with his Son, Jesus Christ. We write this that our joy may be complete. (I John 1:1-4, *Good News for Modern Man.*)

So, if words and actions become, or have seemed to become, a gymnastic, a magical recipe, a secret formula, an intricate legal process, they have become in large effect some foolish, fallible human claptrap that holds us away from him rather than intensifying our union-in-love with him, even though he *is* there, alive in the heart of our confusing, misguided constructions.

We use the terms "real presence" and "transubstantiation" as merely one example. The examples could be multiplied. The document from the *Consultation on Church Union,* "Principles of Church Union, Guidelines for Structure," says,

> We in the United Church must say what we can about the Eucharist, as Christians in every age have struggled to do. Yet we must recognize that human words can never fully express but only point toward redemptive mystery. The church's action

of sharing together in that mystery, in response to the Lord's invitation and command, is altogether more decisive than any effort on our part to think alike about it.[1]

This one table through the bread and the fruit of the vine proclaims the reconciliation accomplished by the death and resurrection of Christ, the longed-for consummation of his victory, and the oneness of the redeemed community. . . . In the Lord's Supper, symbols and symbolic actions are used. However, the Eucharist is an effective sign; the action of the church becomes the effective means whereby God in Christ acts and Christ is present with his people. Our affirmation that the church's Eucharist has effective significance is based upon the promise of Christ as attested in the apostolic church. "This is my body. . . . This is the new covenant in my blood. . . . Do this in remembrance of me." [2]

Responding now to the kindly challenge in the last chapter, I rather happily accept Dr. Garrison's suggestion that I address a remark or two to post-Tridentine Roman Catholic attitudes in view of Vatican II and the rapid developments in Roman Catholicism since that time.

First of all, are we not in a position to agree that councils, like many major religious events, are to be understood in their historical context? They do not absolutize the state of the church so that progress and development of thought are counter-indicated. Now I have said what you may consider an extraordinary statement from a Roman Catholic, and perhaps we may for the moment let that matter rest.

Regarding the specific question of Trent and the concept

---

[1] *Consultation on Church Union* (Cincinnati, Ohio: "Forward" Movement Publications, 1967), p. 48.

[2] *Ibid.*, pp. 48-49.

of sacrifice, it is again the contemporary world that gives us our clearest insight. Before turning to that, however, let us make a strong distinction in our thinking between the official statements of a council and the considerable theologizing that surrounds it.

I, for one, would like to register some Roman Catholic horror at the spate of deplorable theories (not the men, who must have been sincere, dedicated, and well-intentioned) regarding the sacrificial nature of the Eucharist that flooded the theological scene at the time. Many highly esteemed theologians saw the sacrificial aspect of immolation in everything from the separated species of bread and wine, or the consumption of them, or the breaking of the bread, to a *status declivioris,* i.e., a more lowly state that Christ would be considered to have in the Eucharist. But I repeat and would like to do so with considerable emphasis, these were theologians plying their trade: theologizing. Certainly they were free to do so, in fact, should always do so, and we must assume nothing but good faith, and encourage contemporary efforts. However, such ideas represent individual opinion or, at most, a school of thought, not an official, settled, doctrinal consensus or position of a church.

Considering the doctrinal position of Trent and attempting to interpret it, let us now return to that promised contemporary insight. I have in mind specifically the current 1967-68 discussions, particularly those between Lutherans and Roman Catholics and those between Anglicans and Roman Catholics, in the U.S.A. One would expect a greater degree of agreement in the Anglo-Roman discussions regarding the sacrificial nature of the Eucharist, but it is the joint statement of the Lutheran-Roman Catholics that is significantly more specific and stronger. Both final documents are statements of essential agreement in areas that had been assumed almost irreconcilably divisive. On the aspect of sacrifice there is complete accord!

There is neither time nor space here to quote the gratefully received Anglo-Roman statement in detail. You read what was said at Milwaukee in May of 1967. One sentence here will suffice: "Whatever doctrinal disagreements may remain between our Churches, the understanding of the sacrificial nature of the Eucharist is not among them."

But even more significant for our present purpose is the Lutheran-Roman Catholic statement. For example:

> The Catholic affirmation that the church "offers Christ" in the mass has in the course of the last half century been increasingly explained in terms which answer Lutheran fears that this detracts from the full sufficiency of Christ's sacrifice. The members of the body of Christ are united through Christ with God and with one another in such a way that they become participants in his worship, his self-offering, his sacrifice to the Father. Through this union between Christ and Christians, the eucharistic assembly "offers Christ" by consenting in the power of the Holy Spirit to be offered by him to the Father. Apart from Christ we have no gifts, no worship, no sacrifice of our own to offer to God. All we can plead is Christ, the sacrificial lamb and victim whom the Father himself has given us.[3]

It can thus be seen that there is agreement on the "that," the full reality of Christ's presence. What has been disputed is a particular way of stating the "how," the manner in which he becomes present.

Today, however, when Lutheran theologians read contemporary Catholic expositions, it becomes clear to them that the dogma

[3] *Unity Trends* (New York: National Council of Churches, Dept. of Faith and Order [Feb. 15, 1968]), I, 7. Reprinted by permission.

of transubstantiation intends to affirm the fact of Christ's presence and of the change which takes place, and is not an attempt to explain how Christ becomes present. When the dogma is understood in this way, Lutherans find that they also must acknowledge that it is a legitimate way of attempting to express the mystery, even though they continue to believe that the conceptuality associated with "transubstantiation" is misleading and therefore prefer to avoid the term.

On the two major issues which we have discussed at length, however, the progress has been immense. Despite all remaining differences in the ways we speak and think of the eucharistic sacrifice and our Lord's presence in his supper, we are no longer able to regard ourselves as divided in the one, holy, catholic and apostolic faith on these two points. We therefore prayerfully ask our fellow Lutherans and Catholics to examine their consciences and root out many ways of thinking, speaking and acting, both individually and as churches, which have obscured their unity in Christ on these as on many other matters.[4]

These are enormously important advances. And I think they answer Dr. Garrison's questions from the preceding chapter and thus, perhaps, those of many of the major Protestant denominations.

We can perhaps summarize quite neatly within our own present sacramental context in this book: The Eucharist is sacrifice as sacrament. Christ is not immolated again. His sacrifice was perfected once and for all. The virtue of it, however, remains always, and our eucharists re-present this for us. As other sacraments re-present various saving events of Christ, so does the Eucharist for his sacrifice.

In other words, the Eucharist is sacrifice only because it is sacrament.

[4] *Ibid.*, pp. 9, 10.

As we come to greater understanding and consensus in the meaning of the Eucharist in these days of ecumenism, something needs to be said on the question of more open communion between the churches now.

Since the Eucharist is the sacrament of fullest expression of unity-in-love, it is probably more honest not to be able to share the sacrament with total and unrestrained openness —yet. If the churches are not, in fact, capable to the fullest degree of union and love as yet and are officially, at least, divided still, to celebrate the sign as if they were could be misleading. However, as Vatican Council II noted, sacraments are means of grace as well as signs. Some more open communion discipline, at least in certain circumstances, does seem desirable. We must perhaps work toward this. Until we do, and until we achieve greater unity, it will hurt us, particularly at gatherings such as this, not to be able to share the Eucharist together. But perhaps this is part of the price we must pay for the final achievement of greater unity.

Here I must quote Vatican Council documents again. I think they are frequently great, even though, since they are documents and not popular treatments, they demand studied attention rather than casual scanning. I shall conclude this chapter with a quick catalogue of some statements on the Eucharist. This can both summarize what we have said and outline some of the actualities the Eucharist can be for us.

For example, concerning the Eucharist as a basis for Christian community and source of building it up:

No Christian community, however, can be built up unless it has its basis and center in the celebration of the most Holy Eucharist. Here, therefore, all education in the spirit of community must originate. If this celebration is to be sincere and

81

thorough, it must lead to various works of charity and mutual help, as well as to missionary activity and to different forms of Christian witness.[5]

And to reflect what the Eucharist is, even if we do not know it well enough:

The renewal in the Eucharist of the covenant between the Lord and man draws the faithful into the compelling love of Christ and sets them afire. From the liturgy, therefore, and especially from the Eucharist, as from a fountain, grace is channeled into us; and the santification of men in Christ and the glorification of God, to which all other activities of the Church are directed as toward their goal, are most powerfully achieved.[6]

What the Eucharist should be for Christians:

The Lord left behind a pledge of this hope and strength for life's journey in that sacrament of faith where natural elements refined by man are changed into His glorified Body and Blood, providing a meal of brotherly solidarity and a foretaste of the heavenly banquet.[7]

How we all are taken up into him and one another:

Truly partaking of the body of the Lord in the breaking of the Eucharistic bread, we are taken up into communion with Him and with one another. "Because the bread is one, we though many, are one body, all of us who partake of the one bread" (I Cor. 10:17). In this way all of us are made members of His

---

[5] *The Documents of Vatican II*, "Priests," No. 6, pp. 545-46.
[6] *Ibid.*, "Liturgy," No. 10, pp. 142-43.
[7] *Ibid.*, "The Church Today," No. 38, pp. 236-37.

body (cf. I Cor. 12:27), "but severally members one of another" (Rom. 12:5).[8]

How all we have said and will yet attempt to say in this series of ideas on sacraments really originates and terminates in the Eucharist:

Hence the Eucharist shows itself to be the source and the apex of the whole work of preaching the gospel. Those under instruction are introduced by stages to a sharing in the Eucharist. The faithful, already marked with the sacred seal of baptism and confirmation, are through the reception of the Eucharist fully joined to the Body of Christ.[9]

The following says it too, as it points to ecumenism and ties in our original thesis on "God's Sacramental Starting Point":

What has revealed the love of God among us is that the only-begotten Son of God has been sent by the Father into the world, so that, being made man, the Son might by His redemption of the entire human race give new life to it and unify it (cf. I John 4:9; Col. 1:18-20; John 11:52). Before offering Himself up as a spotless victim upon the altar of the cross, He prayed to His Father for those who believe: "That all may be one even as thou, Father, in me, and I in thee; that they also may be one in us, that the world may believe that thou hast sent me" (John 17:21). In His Church He instituted the wonderful sacrament of the Eucharist by which the unity of the Church is both signified and brought about. He gave His followers a new commandment of mutual love (cf. John 13:34),

[8] *Ibid.,* "The Church," No. 7, p. 20.
[9] *Ibid.,* "Priests," No. 5, p. 542.

and promised the Spirit, their Advocate (cf. John 16:7), who, as Lord and life-giver, would abide with them forever.[10]

An added note states:

> Before this final version [of the Council document], the title of the chapter had been "Principles of Catholic Ecumenism." The change implies that the Council recognizes ecumenism as one movement for all Christian Churches and Communities. The goal for all is the same, unity in the Christian faith, but the way of conceiving that unity and faith may vary, and so one may speak of a Church having its own principles of ecumenism. The first section of Chapter I gives a brief statement of beliefs that Catholics bring with them to the dialogue.

Since our unity is not only "signified," but *"brought about"* in the Eucharist by the action of the Spirit, we may, although not yet aware of it, be growing in unity far more than we can imagine at the present moment. Certainly, looking toward the Eucharist, in particular, we should have a daily prayer on our lips and in our hearts, a prayer modeled on his discourse with the apostles the night he gave us the Eucharist:

> "Father, that we may be one,
> as you and the Son are one—
> that we may be one in you;
> then perhaps the world will
> see and believe that you
> have really sent us."

---

[10] *Ibid.*, "Catholic Principles on Ecumenism," No. 2, p. 343.

[7]

THE LOST SACRAMENTS

By the "lost sacraments" we mean the five specifically designated as sacraments and overtly observed as such by Roman Catholics but not by Protestants: (1) Confirmation (dealt with in Chaps. III and IV), (2) Penance, (3) Holy Matrimony, (4) Holy Orders or Ordination, and (5) Extreme Unction, or more broadly, Anointing.

Three usual criteria or liturgical litmus tests applied by Protestantism to determine whether the sacral act is a sacramental act are:

(1) The act must have been instituted by Jesus (by which we have usually meant: clearly commanded by him). In this, Catholic brethren agree, although, so far as I can discover, the teaching authority of Rome has never clearly designated precisely what or which he instituted.

(2) Additionally, a sacrament is "an outward and visible sign of an inward and spiritual grace." Here again, agreement. We shall note shortly some important efforts to qualify this definition or, rather, to hold that it is too qualified and restricting. Here we shall note only that this definition seems

to betray an unbiblical dualism and separation between outer and inner, material and spiritual.

(3) The sacrament is necessary to salvation—although here I demur with a gentle reminder that we should be always on guard against presumptuous pronouncements about what God can or will not do in and for us and others. Nevertheless, one does not have to be ordained in order to be a Christian. Indeed some, both ordained and unordained, even protest that ordination augments the difficulties! Again, one does not necessarily need to be married in order to be yoked to Christ, though some of us want to witness that we have experienced more of judgment upon our selfishness, known more of grace, found more of forgiveness in marriage than in any other human relationship. Still, the Heavenly City must have some bachelor's quarters! Anyway, these are the usual criteria (historical, doctrinal, experiential) for defining the sacraments among Protestants: (1) instituted by Jesus, (2) outward sign —inward grace, (3) necessary to salvation.

I have recently come across what strikes me as an important and promising effort to qualify or broaden these criteria. It is found in the previously referred to volume by Hardin, Quillian, and White. "The principal basis for the validity of the sacraments, however, is the very nature of the whole of his gospel to which the entire Scriptures and the life of the church attest." [1] The biblical tests are here taken quite seriously as in the past but, in harmony with modern biblical scholarship, the Bible is seen as the expression of the gospel, not as the source of it. Moreover, the phrase, "his gospel to which . . . the life of the church attest[s]," makes room for the Christian tradition as at least a subordinate, if not a co-

[1] *The Celebration of the Gospel*, p. 111.

ordinate, factor in the church's self-understanding. This latter provision for vital interaction between scripture and tradition harbors considerable ecumenical promise.

Aside from sacramental definitions and specific designations, Protestants observe *in some form* most of, if not all, the lost sacraments. Try to convince any pastoral counselor that some Protestants do not have (and many more need) their own form of the confessional. Observe the increasing requests on the part of sensitive young couples to place their matrimonial vows consciously within the broader context of corporate worship. Mark the holy, almost luminous significance Protestants have always given to ordination. With the partial exception of extreme unction, Protestants have lost these five sacraments only in the sense that they have subordinated them and declined to call them sacraments.

I

So seen, what are the elements making up a Protestant overview of the lost sacraments? What would assist us in restoring them to a less lost place in what Father Fiedler will propose as a "hierarchy of sacraments."

Stephen Leacock observes somewhere that a college professor is a chap who has to back up at least two thousand years to get a running start on any subject. I shall not back up quite that far, but it is necessary to step back a bit in order to gain some historical perspective. Until the twelfth century all outward signs in the church's life were apparently called simply "sacraments." Then Peter Lombard introduced the distinction (still in use) between his church's seven sacraments and other sacred symbolic acts which are called sacramentals (the sign of the cross, genuflection, sacred images, etc.).

If I may presume for a minute to be an embryonic "Benjamin of Lombardy," I would suggest that Peter Lombard's distinction between sacraments and sacramentals is roughly parallel to the distinction and relationship I am drawing between the five lost sacraments and the traditional basic two. I emphasize "roughly" parallel. The parallel breaks down when one comes to know that Christ is really present in the covenanted relationship of a Christian marriage (personally I should say, sacramentally present). Again absolute distinctions between "sacraments greater" and "sacraments lesser" are difficult to maintain after one has experienced the grace of presence at the ordination altar. Still, I think Peter Lombard's differentiation is helpful: for Protestants, baptism and the Eucharist are sacraments; the other five are sacramentals.

Sacramental theology is at base "sign theology." Yet the function of the sign is to point and—crucial matter—*to point beyond itself*. Here we, Reformed and Roman alike, have sinned against this holy law of sacramental theology almost unforgivably. Sketched parabolically, the sin looks something like this:

Suppose a road sign reads, "Austin 45 miles." The purpose of the sign is to get us to travel to Austin. What have we in the church done with our various sacramental signs (and I might add, equally with our creeds)? We have admired their beauty and have expended considerable precious energy and treasure keeping them in good repair. We have built little rustic rubric fences around them, planted liturgical grass at their base, maybe even put little bronze placques on them to indicate when they were erected and by whom. In short, or rather, at length, we have treated the signs as if they were themselves important and consequently have neglected to undertake the journey.

Confession: the journey to penitence. Penance: the journey motivated by penitence. Matrimony: the joint journey encircled by a love that binds man to woman and both to God. Ordination: a march in the midst of a people. Extreme Unction: a journey into death, certified and sustained by him who conquered it. Sacraments, major or minor, gain their point and maintain their meaning only by reason of *whom* they point to.

Another way of indicating the "in motion" nature of sacramental theology is to say that it is an enacted one: a theology centered in act. The sacraments are the church's way of italicizing the saving Word: penance is his way now of pronouncing, "Neither do I condemn you, go, and do not sin again" (John 8:11). Holy Matrimony is his way today of blessing a union as he did first at Cana. Holy Orders are the contemporary modes of his being among us as "one who serves" (symbolized vividly in the stole, the badge of ordination, and the stylized descendants of the servant's sweat towel). Last rites are the everlasting arms reaching across the chasm of death, steadying the soul for its final step toward that house not made with hands.

I noted earlier an implied Protestant re-definition of the sacraments. The English Jesuit Bernard Leeming, has attempted another from his perspective: "Might not a sacrament be better defined as 'an effective sign of a particular form of union with . . . the Church, instituted by Jesus Christ, which gives grace to those who receive it rightly'? " [2] Whether or not that is accepted as sufficiently definitive, it nevertheless contains an important nugget of truth, namely, besides being signs of the presence of Christ, these lost sacraments are signs

---

[2] Quoted by Diekmann, *Come, Let Us Worship,* p. 48.

of the faith of the church: its faith that the cleansed life is a new life (penance); that the married life can be a means of grace (holy matrimony); that human beings can share in the priesthood of Christ (ordination); that mortality is semifinal, not complete (extreme unction).

Furthermore these final five sacraments derive their meanings from the basic two. What baptism imparts penance extends, matrimony utilizes, ordination intensifies, and extreme unction seals. Their relationships to the Eucharist are closer still. Each sacrament is a eucharistic echo. Or, as Schillebeeckx puts it, "Every sacrament is a personal presence of Christ." [3] And a means by which he is present for a particular purpose: to cleanse (penance), to unify (matrimony), to serve (ordination), and to sustain (extreme unction).

Seen, then, as encounters with Christ, these sacraments are lost or neglected only to our own impoverishment.

II

Protestants, as we know, have no sacrament of *penance.* That sacrament strictly consists of repentance, confession to a priest (usually), satisfaction as imposed by the confessor, and absolution. Yet if Bonhoeffer was correct when, in his little book *Life Together,* he held that the power to forgive sins belongs to the Christian as Christian, we *ought* to have such an ordinance. Catholics have made the bad mistake of restricting the power of forgiveness to the ordained priesthood. Protestants have made the worse mistake of not exercising it at all.

The practice of private confession to a priest apparently arose in Ireland. It was not at first a part of the sacrament of

[3] *Christ the Sacrament of the Encounter with God,* p. 60.

penance. In fact it was an early form of "pastoral counseling" designed to give religious guidance and brotherly correction to monks. Many present-day priests are ready to say that *in this regard,* that is, for personal guidance and correction, the confessional is a kind of patent medicine and not a markedly curative kind. It should be said, however, that the confessional may meet other needs adequately, for instance, the need to be heard or the need for absolution.

Yet somehow I am not quite able to dismiss the whole practice with a cavalier arch of my Reformed eyebrows. When the sullied and brokenhearted penitent cries out, in words or in groanings too deep for words, "But what can I *do!"* we serve him ill if we permit the doctrine of salvation by grace to blunt the poignancy of his needy cry. Maybe God does *not* require whatever it is that the penitent feels the need to do, but the penitent *does,* and he should not therefore be sent empty away.

Not that private confession is without its dangers. One of them is that it is dominated (perhaps inevitably) by one's *conscious* sins, whereas (if my own experience is any test) my worst sins are not always my felt ones. When I am unjustly angry, I know it. When I indulge in lustful thought or bear false witness or fail to bear any witness at all, I am usually quite uncomfortably aware of these facts (these sins). But the real damage is done when my self-preference is so habitual or intense that I do not even know it, even when I am told. The harsher affront occurs when I exploit my brothers but convince myself (and occasionally maybe even convince them) that I am serving them.

The second danger stems from the first: In the concentrating upon my identifiable sins I am in danger, in Carlyle's indelicate and not altogether accurate phrase about the early

Methodists, of spending too much time contemplating my spiritual navel.

The common form of confession in the Reformed churches is corporate. This is an absolutely indispensable aspect, a positively crucial context, of confession for the people of God. My sins are seldom solitary. My loves are never alone. "*We* have offended against Thy holy laws." Even without the plural "we," it should be clear that "laws" are an imperative laid upon a people and that offenses against the laws are offenses against that people. Because God is the people's Sovereign, the offenses are against him, too. But, as we observed in Chap. I, one of man's basic defining needs is for community. Corporate confession, even in its form, is a symbolic recognition that we, each and all, have hobbled and crippled ourselves and thus have threatened our very family nature.

Nevertheless the General Confession, though necessary, is almost always too general. Sometimes while trying to pray it, and having wandered from my own confession, I am tempted to halt my people with a challenge: Which desires of your own heart have you followed too much, John? For academic promotion? For civilized revenge? Which of God's holy laws have you offended against, Mary? False witness? Coveting? And you there, whose name (I confess) I do not know: What have you left undone that you ought to have done—precisely now and specifically? General confession, if we are not very alert, can be a means of escape instead of a means of grace. Contrition, the old Latin word, means the state of being crushed. When this aspect is absent, confession itself usually is.

The opening verses of the thirty-second Psalm express quite pointedly the need for confession, without which man faces the very destruction of his personality.[4] When the psalmist "declared not his sin," his "strength was dried up as by the heat of summer" (v. 4).

For all the limitations of private confession I am nonetheless convinced that we could well take a page from the breviary of our brethren. We need *something* quite as specific as the confessional—in sin confessed, in forgiveness pronounced. I have often been almost covetous of my priest-brothers' capacity to send a penitent away—restored, renewed, and reconciled—with a convincing assurance which no pastoral counseling (particularly of the so-called "non-directive" sort) can either claim or accomplish.

Let me illustrate. Some years ago a young woman came to me tortured with the guilt born with her illegitimate child, compounded by the cankerous secret kept even from the father of the child. I listened long. I spoke of what *I* knew of the forgiving grace of God. I wrapped both the time for speaking and the time for keeping silent in what *I* thought were the luminous, revealing veils of scripture, to no avail. Finally, moved by an unmistakable prompting, I took her to the chapel and knelt with her in prayer. Then I stood while she still knelt, placed my hand upon her head and said, "Rebecca" (this is, of course, not her name), "Rebecca, I forgive you in the name of God. Now go, and live as a forgiven woman." I could tell you of the creative, restorative consequences in her life, but that is not my present point. My point is that we Protestants need some such pointed, specific, tangible counterpart to the Roman confessional.

In fact, what we need (but here the "we" includes the whole church) is to hold together both the private and

---

[4] See Lawrence E. Toombs, *The Old Testament in Christian Preaching* (Philadelphia: Westminster Press, 1961), p. 172.

the public, the individual and the common. This was made quite clear to me recently by one of my dearest friends. She is a nun of the delightfully liberated, slightly impish, completely "en-Christed" variety. She said to me, as we left Mass together, "How I envy you your corporate confession! So full of the sense of community. I get so tired being told that sin is only anger at my superior, or wanting a modern habit to wear, or missing Mass" (she never does). The penitential grass, it seems, is always greener on the other side of the confessional!

Anyway, in some such manner we may be enabled to remember that penance is an extension of baptism, "a second plank after shipwreck," as Jerome put it. It results in a reconciliation which offers both an upward thrust and an outward grasp. It comes, as even Thomas Aquinas insists, because "God alone absolves from sin and forgives sin absolutely." [5] But it *comes,* and with it something akin to what Wesley called "the New Birth."

III

Nowhere has the church vitiated our given gospel more than in our practices, or malpractices, of *matrimony.* (Our sacramental sins are so serious that I am hesitant to add the usual adjective "holy.") People we have never seen before come to the clergyman, often at the last minute, after the gown is chosen, the date selected, and the invitations all but printed, and "want to be married, Reverend." Why? Oh, for the profound reason that the Reverend's church building has the largest nave in the county, or the chancel will decorate prettily, or the church is nearby, or Susie was married here

[5] *Summa Theologica* III. 84.3, Response, ad. obj. 3.

and liked the organ music so *very* much. Then, sometimes, with little or no effort at preparation, we permit them to take upon their lips what are perhaps the most unequivocal vows in the English language, in a service laden with religious, specifically with Christian, assumptions, which they have not even examined, let alone affirmed. And all this in the name of a "church wedding," if you will excuse the term.

May God have mercy on our souls.

In this burlesque appears no slightest awareness that, as Bishop Sheen states it, it takes "Three To Get Married" (he rather understates it, for marriage takes place within a community). I am not challenging the right of these persons to be married on such minimal terms. I am denying the right of the church to bless such a marriage.

No wonder such transient hopefuls succeed in overlooking the solidly symbolic nature of the whole service. Talk about "en-acted" theology! It is more than mildly amusing to observe the very "Protestant" type of Protestant who thinks that genuflecting is a Catholic plot—it is amusing to watch him participate in a liturgy so loaded with symbolism: Hands joined and clasped; rings given and received; knees bent and head bowed; even the kiss. All these are, or are meant to be, outward signs of inward grace. They are symbolic and message-laden to the core.

The minister really does not validate a marriage. He seals it with the church's blessing. The Catholic priest, for example, declares: "By the authority of the church I ratify and bless the bond of marriage which you have contracted." If a bomb were to drop on the church building an instant after a couple have pledged their troth but before I had pronounced them "one in marriage," I do not know what the law would say but I would bury them as man and wife.

But notice well: What is required for a valid Christian marriage is not the presence of a pastor but the presence of Christ—which thrusts us right back again upon its sacramental nature. Marriage is a particular kind of encounter with Christ. In the presence of each other these two are to find a divine Third. We should not literalize the life out of this. When a man embraces his wife in the marital bed, he need not—probably cannot—*consciously* think in liturgical terms. That would be expecting a bit too much of human frailty! The bed is *not* an altar, after all. Nevertheless, in a Christian marriage both he and she can face with faith and confidence all the anxieties, uncertainties, tragedies; all the delights, joys, and peace which lie ahead. So it is in a sacramental marriage.

IV

Greater brevity in this section is in order because at least one important aspect of *ordination* is to be dealt with in Chap. IX.

It has been pointed out that the New Testament word for order (or ordination), the word *taxis,* refers to the redeployment of troops from a marching to a battle formation. Various orders or ordinations are intended to enable the church more effectively to engage in combat. Thus: Ordination is a method of deployment: "Some should be apostles, some prophets, some evangelists, . . . pastors, . . . teachers . . ." (Eph. 4:11).

What ancient ordinations would be abolished, what new ones established on this battle basis?

Does this not provide at least some rationale for a doctrine of apostolic succession? Granted, as Wesley insisted, that no unbroken succession back to the beginning is either observable or provable. Granted further that apostolic succession cannot be equated with tactual succession and that those who truly stand in the succession of the apostles are those who proclaim what the apostles proclaimed. Still, is it not the case that those who reject the doctrine (quite understandably as it is sometimes interpreted) are nevertheless obliged to see in it a valid principle of order (of troop deployment) or, if not able to see that, to suggest an alternate and better one?

Particularly is this the case when one considers the chaos with which a rampantly Protestant concept "of order" (strange term under the circumstances) burdens us. Could any conceivable doctrinal "straitjacket" imposed by a mechanistic insistence upon apostlic succession be any more deplorable or disastrous than that formless freedom which sometimes hides under the name of Protestant? Driving through West Virginia I passed a little building marked, strangely, "The Church of the Speckled Bird," for no better reason than that some dear, sincere, but nutty soul had misread the prophet Jeremiah, "Is my heritage to me like a speckled bird . . ." (chap. 12, v. 9)? No Roman Catholic, believe me, could possibly have been more appalled than I. At that moment I would have given a great deal for a little order!

The point to be remembered, pondered, and acted upon (order or no order) is that all our ministries are incomplete and will be, so long as they are launched and carried on in isolation from one another. This is an empirical (I would say even a verifiable) fact, whatever our doctrines of ministry. Without mine, Father Fiedler's ministry is imperfect; without his, mine is deficient. Whatever I must do to correct this fragmentation, I am obliged, in obedience to Christ, gladly to seek, resolutely to embrace, and fully to share.

It may come as some surprise to "Free Church" Christians

to be reminded that their Old New England congregations, so stalwart in their resistance to any minister assigned to them by outside authority, did not in fact elect their ministers. They voted for them but only as a means of nominating them to Christ.[6] Whatever the practical difficulties in deploying, controlling, or even recognizing such a priesthood, this is the essential perspective which must be beneath all our ordinations. No bishop however exalted, no congregation however free, makes a priest. Only an encounter with Christ can do that, sacramentally.

V

The sacrament of anointing will be harder to interpret, let alone to appropriate, in any meaningful Protestant terms. Only a slender minority of Protestants practice or possess anything like this sacrament.

A slight but slowly growing number of Protestants anoint the sick or practice the laying on of hands. With a few important exceptions, however, we have permitted the ministry of healing to fall into the hands of sectarians who have truncated the whole gospel by exaggerating one part of it; or we have given this spiritual treasury over to the coffers of the quacks. The resulting judgment upon us may be more severe than upon the sectarians or the quacks, for they would never have had the opportunity for profiteering exploitation if central stream churches had kept closer to their New Testament and to the healing gospel of the Great Physician.

A few Episcopalians, almost alone among non-Roman Christians, have kept the healing faith for the rest of us. *The*

[6] See Douglas Horton, *The Meaning of Worship* (New York: Harper & Bro., 1959), p. 111.

Book of Common Prayer provides for the "Unction of the Sick" under the following rubric:

> When any sick person shall in humble faith desire the ministry of healing through Anointing or Laying on of Hands, the Minister may use such portions of the foregoing Office as he shall think fit, and the following:

> O Blessed Redeemer, relieve, we beseech thee, by thy indwelling power, the distress of this thy servant; release him from sin, and drive away all pain of soul and body, that being restored to soundness of health he may offer thee praise and thanksgiving; who livest and reignest with the Father and the Holy Ghost, one God, world without end. Amen.

> I anoint thee with oil (or I lay my hand upon thee), in the name of the Father, (and of the Son, and of the Holy Ghost; beseeching the mercy of our Lord Jesus Christ, that all thy pain and sickness of body being put to flight, the blessing of health may be restored unto thee. Amen.

Methodists might note that, in his *Notes on the New Testament*, Wesley refers with approval to the apostles' practice of anointing the sick, objecting only in the later restriction of it to a deathbed rite, a restriction some contemporary Roman Catholics object to and are attempting to reverse. Furthermore, both Wesleys refer in their journals to administering Holy Communion to the sick or dying.[7] This would appear to be an effort to provide some kind of experiential equivalent.

[7] John Wesley, *Journal*, June 10, 1763; Charles Wesley, *Journal*, November 3, 1740; May 8, 1744; and July 9, 1750.

I have tried to show in this chapter that the "Lost Sacraments" are intended to address us at the point of real and, except for the last, recurrent needs and then to bear to us the saving Presence who meets those needs. Doctrinal questions aside, the church is bound to attempt this, if she is to take seriously the sacramental nature of life and of death and of the faith that redemptively unites them.

[8]

A HIERARCHY OF
SACRAMENTS?

Clearly something needs to be said about the number of sacraments. And it is also clear that I am the member of the team who must say it. This too may not be as formidable a problem as it at first seems.

Particularly at the grass roots pastoral level, it would seem that interesting discoveries are being made today. Recently, for example, in a small, local ministerial association which meets regularly for theological discussions, the subject of Christian marriage was studied. The aspect of its possible sacramentality was inevitably a part of the discussion. The Methodist pastor remarked to his Roman Catholic brother that there were going to be inescapable and perhaps insurmountable differences here since the Methodist doctrine did not consider marriage a sacrament, whereas Roman Catholic doctrine did. His friend asked if he believed that Christ was especially present in the celebration of the marriage event. Of course, he was! As the discussion continued, they found that their beliefs about the actual content of the event were

101

practically identical. In one church it was called a sacrament, in the other it was not. This may seem all too simple, yet in such developments, do we not in truth find the spirit of the Lord active and revealing himself among his people—where they actually live? Granted that it is far too simple a general answer for all problems; still, is it not frequently a problem of seemingly canonized semantics and terminology rather than of doctrinal fact?

One of the points of apparent immobility, doctrinally, in the discussion, was the question of the institution of the sacraments. The Roman Catholic position has traditionally seemed to stress the direct institution by Christ of each of the seven sacraments even, for many theologians, as historically provable from Scripture. To this point it is illuminating to hear some of the most prestigious Roman Catholic theologians suggesting alternatives. Karl Rahner, for example, says,

> From the principle that the Church is the primal sacrament it would be possible to see that the existence of true sacraments in the strictest traditional sense is not necessarily and always based on a definite statement, which has been preserved or is presumed to have existed, in which the historical Jesus Christ explicitly spoke about a certain definite sacrament. . . . The institution of a sacrament can (it is not necessarily implied that it must always) follow simply from the fact that Christ founded the Church with its sacramental nature; . . . for only on the basis of the doctrine about the Church, the fundamental sacrament, can the sacramentality of several sacraments be recognized at all.
>
> In order to be clear about scope and significance of what for the moment has only been indicated here, we must ask how it is possible to demonstrate in an historically credible way the sacramentality of matrimony, holy orders, extreme unction and

confirmation, that is to say, here, their institution by Christ, . . .
For four sacraments have no words of institution from Jesus
Christ himself. . . .

But it is just this assumption which is unproved and incorrect
as can be seen from the possible manner of institution of a
sacrament by Christ which we have suggested, namely by
implicit institution of a sacrament in the explicit institution
of the Church as the historically visible form of eschatologically
victorious grace.[1]

For many Protestants, these are, probably, interesting concepts when advanced by a Roman Catholic theologian.

Are there two sacraments? or seven? or ninety-five? or ten
thousand? Broadly speaking and looking at the essential incarnational nature of the church, there are more than either
two or seven. But it has been a traditional controversy between Protestant and Catholic theologians as to whether the
number must be seen as two only or extended to seven. Here,
too, our defensive stances about our traditional utterances have
been too rigid. After all, from the increased understanding
in these days of the church itself, must we not first say that
the essential thing to be maintained about the sacraments is
not the number seven or two but the fact that there are rites
in the church that are of sacramental efficacy? Christ is *the*
sacrament. The number of ways he chooses to manifest himself sacramentally is of secondary importance to that first essential fact. Karl Rahner has equally creative thoughts on this.
Without adding or subtracting anything, the Roman church
could quite easily, even now, suggest to its adherents that
there are nine sacraments, or six sacraments. This could really
be quite easily done, because the Roman sacrament of holy

[1] *The Church and the Sacraments* (New York: Herder and Herder,
1963), pp. 41, 50.

103

orders has several grades to it, specifically diaconate, priesthood, and episcopate. The Roman Church recognizes the sacramentality of diaconate and episcopate—whether they are taken separately or as a whole with priesthood is merely a question of terminology.

Also there is such a lengthy tradition that sees the sacrament of confirmation as a part of the sacramental rite of Christian initiation, that no Roman Catholic theologian would be branded a heretic (if such branding be acceptable in polite society any longer) by asserting that there are six instead of seven sacraments, so long as he admitted that confirmation is truly a sacramental rite.

To speak of sacramental rites and the church in such contexts is surely to place us in a position of potentially more open discussion of the subject. We all accept the fact that Christ has left us certain symbols as viable, simple, trustworthy signs of himself and his continuing living presence among us.

Facing one possible reconciliation of at least partial advance, why not even now suggest a kind of hierarchy of sacraments? Even before the theological work on the essence and individual reality of sacraments is completed by the theologian of an ecumenical age, baptism and the Eucharist are surely admitted as primary sacraments in Christianity. Following the line of thought both of the foregoing concepts of Karl Rahner and of the growing feeling in Protestantism as capsulized in the remarks of Dr. Garrison in the preceding chapter, Protestant thinkers are accepting the idea of the church as the enduring presence of Christ in the world. This is truly the fundamental sacrament, the source of all the sacraments which variously establish his presence in the church. Catholics can surely see the difference in importance of baptism and the Eucharist in relation to the others. Or can they? Do they not do so already? Can we not move on together in our efforts to reach Christ's intentions for us in the church and, removing some of the divisive and unnecessary mishmash, make him more accessible today to the world he comes to love?

After outlining the preceding, I came across a brief but rich article by Yves Congar, O.P., that deserves reference and, in view of our title, demands quotation: "The idea that some sacraments are more important than others, particularly baptism and the Eucharist, is well supported by traditional theology," and, quoting Gregory VII,

> "Holy Church, the mother of all . . . has received several sacraments. There are, however, but a few of them, two given by the Lord himself, others instituted by the Apostles." The reasons for this grading may be found either in the source of the sacraments, namely, Christ, or in the effect of the sacraments on the faithful and the Church.
>
> Baptism and Eucharist are clearly in a position of privilege due to a formal expression of Christ's will, attested by Scripture.
>
> The Council (Vatican II) has also hallowed the description of the Church as the "universal sacrament of salvation." This, together with the concept of People of God, is one of Vatican Council II's richest contributions to ecclesiology. . . .
>
> Within the world the Church is the sign and instrument (Const. on the Church, n. 1.) of that renewal of the world on which God has irrevocably decided and of which the incarnation of his Son inserted the principle into history (ibid., nn. 48, 3). Luther used to speak of two sacraments as instituted by Christ himself. It should be noted that Luther and also the Augsburg Confession always joined an explanation of confession to their teaching on baptism and Eucharist. . . .
>
> Calvin also admitted that one could call sacrament the

imposition of hands by which ministers or pastors were received in office, but he maintained, more firmly than Melanchthon, that there were only two sacraments, basing himself on the criterion of a divine institution attested by Scripture, while he distinguished "the five other ceremonies" from these two, as they were "of a lower degree."

I am aware of the fact that to restore in our theology, and therefore afterwards in our catechetics, the traditional idea of "major" sacraments may risk encouraging the Protestant denial of the proper sacramental quality of the other sacraments. But we have seen that this denial is not absolute, but is limited to the aspect of the immediate and explicit institution by Christ.[2]

Catholics should remember that Vatican II in the Decree on Ecumenism says that there is a certain hierarchy among the truths to be believed and the teachings to be taught.

Considering the essential ideas just mentioned, ideas upon which I believe we would say we essentially agree, why do we continue to tilt with windmills? Do we simply enjoy theological gymnastics? Is it all part of the game to keep shuffling old pieces around the board even after it is evident that the design on them is worn beyond practical recognition? What are the essential ideas?

First: Christ is God's sacrament.
Second: Church is Christ continuing as physically tangible.
Third: Christ did certain things to communicate himself to us.
Fourth: He continues to do so in the church.

[2] Yves Congar, O.P., "The Notion of 'Major' or 'Principal' Sacraments," *Concilium*, XXXI (1968), 21, 24, 28, 31.

Fifth: Some of these actions of Christ were clearly more important than others.

Sixth: They still are.

Very well, after that point, if you care to carry on a numbers game to the extent that it is divisive rather than unifying in love, by all means proceed. But proceed at you own risk. The world is longing to touch Christ and has been shunted off long enough by the cloud of pettiness in a nit-picking that tragically conceals him.

Christ is the essential reality. We have the responsibility to keep his house in order that he may live among us as fully as possible. Some household articles are also articles of clothing and such personal items as eyeglasses. Let us keep his clothing clean and tastefully contemporary. Let us keep the glasses clean so the world can see him as clearly as weakened eyes will allow.

Let us give him that chance to come to us as fully as he may intend without sidetracking the whole marvelous process by continuing to act as children playing hopscotch.

Paul said, "I live, now no longer the worried, proud I, but Christ lives in me!" Let the church, which is you and me, make that statement again with honesty and with great, living faith!

[9]

THE SPOKEN SACRAMENT

One of our modest hopes for this book is that it will help apply the brakes to a highly elastic use of the word "sacrament." One can read or hear of the sacrament of silence, the sacrament of service, the sacrament of sympathy, the sacrament of nature, the sacrament of comradeship, the sacrament of sex. I myself have sometimes been guilty of such poetizing and inaccuracy. It is a noteworthy tribute to the gospel sacraments and to the life principles of which they are the supreme expression that men have used the word and seen the expression in so many different, sometimes contradictory, places.

The phrase "sacrament of preaching" (which is what is intended by this chapter's title, "The Spoken Sacrament") might seem to be one more such voluble usage of the word "sacrament," as difficult to pick up and examine as mercury on the laboratory table and not half so useful. But we think not. It appears to us that much which we have been trying to clarify and affirm in this volume is summed and symbolized in this ancient art-craft-discipline-agony known as preaching. It is the assumption of this chapter that this phrase is descriptive.

I

The very title "Spoken Sacrament" designates the gospel unity of Word and Sacrament. Some sections of the church and segments of her history have emphasized one more than the other, sometimes one to the exclusion of the other, but the gospel itself justifies no such one-sidedness, overemphasis, or subordination.[1]

Karl Barth once made the very interesting and seminal suggestion that every service of worship normatively should open with the sacrament of baptism, hinge on the act of preaching, and swing toward the climax of Holy Communion. The first requirement, baptism, might be a salutary judgment upon our sterile evangelism. Not often, at least not often enough, would we have anybody to baptize! The homiletical requirement needs no urging, in Protestantism at least, leaving aside for the moment whether what passes for preaching really is. The eucharistic requirement would, if not secure, then at least seek the presence promised in baptism and proclaimed in preaching. The practical difficulties of Barth's suggestion are enormous. For one thing, American congregations habituated to worshiping in sixty minute spurts, would be sending out for coffee by the time we reached the *Sursum Corda*. But apart from the logistical problems the intention of the suggestion is in the right direction: to emphasize the unity of Word and sacraments. Stephen F. Winward underlines this unitary nature of the gospel when he writes: "God reveals and communicates himself through His word, spoken

[1] To cite just one instance: Schillebeeckx has insisted that preaching at the Mass is an integral part of the service of the Word, not an interruption: "The entire eucharistic celebration is thus a service of The Word." Edward Schillebeeckx, "Revelation in Word and Deed," *The Word: Readings in Theology* (New York: P. J. Kenedy & Sons, 1964), p. 268.

and visible, uttered and embodied, proclaimed by preacher and by sacraments. To separate either sacrament from the proclamation and acceptance of the gospel is to pervert it." [2]

The sources of the patterns of worship (patterns which at their best are the distillation of Christian experience and the focusing of Christian truth) are two: the synagogue, where the scriptures were read and interpreted, and the Upper Room, where the bread was broken and the cup shared.

Theodore O. Wedel, one of the ablest preachers of the Anglican communion, has called our attention to an interesting biblical word usage, which as he rightly sees is of "significance for a Protestant-Catholic dialogue on this issue" of Word and sacrament, or (unfortunately sometimes) Word *versus* sacrament. He notes that "Paul employs the Greek word for 'preaching' in what is possibly the most important New Testament account of the institution of the Lord's Supper (I. Cor. 11:23-26): "For as often as you eat this bread and drink the cup, you proclaim [preach] the Lord's death until he comes." So, he says, "to rob the ministry of the Word of its importance in order to honor the sacraments is to set up a false alternative." [3] He would agree, I am sure, that it is a false alternative either way. Similarly, the late beloved Pope John reminded some pilgrims of the twin treasures of our faith, the Book and the Cup.

Historically, as we know to our discomfort, the church has not always been so wise. Sometimes the Word has been subordinated (subjugated, actually) to the sacrament and preaching perverted to a mild, harmless, and occasional appendage

---

[2] *The Reformation of Our Worship,* p. 69.

[3] "Is Preaching Outmoded?" *Religion in Life,* XXXIV (Autumn, 1965), 542.

consisting mostly of weightless inanities spun from the preacher's last minute imaginations. Elsewhere the sacrament has been subordinated (subjugated, actually) to the Word, and the Eucharist perverted into a cold, formless, and occasional appendage conducted in whatever sparse time is left over or on those Lord's Days when the chief spokesman is either absent from the parish or just returning from a church meeting.

We should be grateful, therefore, for the energetic efforts to reunite this pair so long disjoined. The World Council of Churches' Commission on Faith and Order stated it succinctly:

> Sermon and Sacrament are complementary. The Sacrament is upheld by, and is the bringing to life of, our Lord's words of institution: the sermon in which God Himself addresses the congregation, though through frail human channels, is an action by means of which God's grace reaches man.[4]

The awesomeness and inescapability of this twin responsibility is burned into the consciousness of the candidate for ordination when, after he has made his vows, the ordaining authority (in the following case a bishop) says to him: "Take thou authority in the Church to preach the Word of God, and to administer the holy sacraments in the congregation. Amen."

Amen indeed! The tradition is old, the authority derivative, the unity really unbreakable. Even Robert Bruce, Scottish Reformer, called "the Word . . . the other part of the Sacra-

---

[4] Edwall, P., *et al.*, eds. *Ways of Worship: The Report of a Theological Commission of Faith and Order* (Harper & Bros., 1951), p. 3.

ment. I mean and understand by 'the Word' . . . that which serves as its soul . . . and gives life to the whole action." [5]

He intends here by the Word not the sermon but the Word behind the sermon and behind the sacrament, that Word of which sermon and sacrament are coordinate and coordinating expressions. As coordinate and coordinating expressions they have been joined together by the church of God and are rent asunder only to the peril and impoverishment of the people they are meant to serve and to save.

I remark here, before proceeding, an irony, from my own peculiar Protestant perspective. At the very time when some Protestants are adding preaching to their mortality lists—that *too* is dead, it is said—Catholics are adding homileticians to their theological faculties. If the situation gets much worse, we may have to send our Reformed seminarians to Catholic seminaries to teach them how, and maybe even what, to preach!

With this as background let us look more closely at this unity from the side of the proclaimed Word.

II

The sermon's *words* proceed from the saving *Word*.

It is here, by inference, that the so-called radical theologians are so nearly right but so radically wrong. Understandably, they do not say very much about preaching. They do not really seem very interested in it. But they do emphasize that what little residue from the faith "modern man" is able to scrape together comes from Jesus, the fleshed-out Word from God, or former God. Whatever little bit man can now perceive and believe, hear and heed, live toward and die for, is caught in the Galilean accents of Jesus of Nazareth.

[5] *The Mystery of the Lord's Supper,* pp. 62-63.

112

They cannot really have it that way, of course, and some-times I suspect that, uneasily, they know they cannot. If God is dead then the Jesus-faith in God is mortally and deservedly wounded, and is not long for even *this* world. But that way lies no Jesus! You cannot find him, let alone follow him without the faith that sustained and impelled him. One may judge him to have been deluded in that faith, but one may not separate him from it without doing violence to both.

Yet somehow I cannot but admire these men, in spite of myself. However faulty their logic, however violently they have severed their theological taproots, they are still endeav-oring to take Jesus with high seriousness. Orthodoxy of what-ever variety, Nicene, Neo-, or any other, gives us a Christ so ethereal and unearthly, so transcendent and unavailable that, though you could perhaps worship him, you could not follow him. Liberalism of whatever variety, continental, recon-structed, or any other, gave us a Jesus so pale and practical, so immanent and available that, though you could follow him, you could not worship him. These men at least have a *reality* on their hands. There is, I insist, a less violent way to arrive at him who is the *real* Word, but let us not deny them their due.

In order to move toward what I mean by the assertion that the sermon's words proceed from the saving Word, I invite you to ponder again that inexhaustibly perplexing, ineffably revealing event known as the Petrine confession. Jesus and the twelve are in the city earlier called Paneas for the god Pan, more recently bearing the compound name Caesarea Philippi for Caesar and his local functionary. Perhaps Jesus had come slowly to sense that his hour was near and that it was there-fore time to take his disciples more closely into his confidence. For whatever reason, he indulged himself in that very human

113

question, "What do people think of me?" or, as Mark phrases it, "Who do men say that I am?"

Like most friends, they do not tell him immediately what *they* think. Rather, they repeat the rumors, what the grapevine says. One version had it that he was John the Baptizer (the local authorities were superstitiously frantic lest the recently executed John should return to haunt them). Others, with more insight, thought he might be the prophet Jeremiah. Then, softly, came the clincher question: "But what do *you* think?"

That one they could not dodge or escape or quote an answer to or footnote. The Synoptics do not tell us for sure, but at this point I should imagine: silence, except in the big, pounding heart of Peter. He had always been the impulsive one, as a result of which we have from his lips some of the most stupid as well as some of the most profound statements in the New Testament.

"Well," he must have thought, "why shouldn't I say it? I've been thinking it for quite a while now." Thus what had begun as an intuition, as tender as the roots of an olive tree, was born as an affirmation, rushing to his lips and leaping out into the oriental air with all the urgency of a runner announcing a victory. "*You—are—the Christ!*" Now it was said. The Word had found words.

If that were all that preaching were required to say or to contend with, it would be an easier enterprise. But note quite carefully that an instant later Blessed Peter, so full of faith, was the object of an ire so scalding and a judgment so severe that he would never again be able to think of Caesarea Philippi without wincing in shame. Having affirmed that his master was the Anointed One of God, he protested Jesus' counter-affirmation that this anointing would involve and require

114

suffering. So it is just four verses from the triumphant cry, "You are the Christ," to the tragic denunciation, "Get behind me, Satan!" (You are the devil!)

The preaching of the gospel lives in the tension between its confession of faith and its confession of failure. If it is often very difficult to confess the one: "You are the Christ," it is more difficult still to admit the other: "You are the devil." In the preaching of the gospel these words about the Word assume flesh and dwell among a people, full of grace and truth.

This happens just rarely enough to keep us humble and just often enough to keep us going.

III

Again, these *words* about the *Word* are proclaimed by a stammering saint.

Chekhov said something about writers which should be a source of profound encouragement to preachers: "There are big dogs and small dogs, and the small ones need not be put out by the existence of the big ones. All of them have a duty to bark—to bark with whatever voice God has given." [6]

Which is to say that the stammering saint, the dog who barks for God, is a man. How tired he gets being treated as if he were a part of some previously undiscovered third sex, neither male nor female nor honestly neuter, a kind of male virgin Mary upon whom the bishop laid but one hand at ordination, and that lightly. Bishop Edmund S. Janes once offered the reminder that "ministers are good men, but they are men." [7] So be it!

[6] Quoted by Ivan Bunin in "Chekhov," *Atlantic Monthly* (July 1951), p. 60.

[7] Henry B. Ridgaway, *The Life of Edmund S. Janes* (Cincinnati: Phillips and Hunt, 1882), p. 174.

Until Father Fiedler clarified it, I had not been quite clear about the precise meaning of the sacramental doctrine of *ex opere operato,* the contention that the sacraments unfailingly convey grace. The worthiness of the celebrant and the intention of the recipient are secondary. Such a mechanistic, almost magical interpretation, however widespread in the sixteenth century or since, fails to do justice to the careful qualifications in the teachings of the church, some of the nuances and subtleties of which no doubt are still escaping me.

Nevertheless, even as baldly stated, as a preacher I take not a little comfort from the general idea. If a man had unfailingly to be what he is commissioned obediently to proclaim, who then could preach? If the grace of God had no originating power to pervade and transcend the failures, falterings, and sins through which and by whom it is proclaimed, where then is the grace? If the God of grace cannot overrule and yet use his ministers of grace, where is the gospel? The sacrament of preaching does convey what it promises, not quite independent of us but sometimes quite in spite of us.

I have a pained recollection from my first pastorate. A young woman and good friend, in sharp pangs of grief at the sudden death of her father, lashed out at my admittedly too easy words of comfort. "How would you know?" she cried, "You haven't lost your father!" That would not have been the moment to counter with a systematic theology for sorrow even if I had had the presence of mind for it. But several weeks later I said to her, "Virginia, a minister is only the channel, not the source, of the life and gospel he tries to share." Which is to say, in our terms, that our words about the Word are sometimes proclaimed through stammering lips. In fact, usually.

116

Yet we can do no other. You may recall that passage from Cecil S. Forester's novel of the sea, *The Good Shepherd,* which came out of World War II. During one of the endless and often fatal U-boat watches in the North Atlantic, the ship's captain watches a young signal corpsman bending over his instrument panel. The commander observes that the youth is fresh out of boot camp, yet it is his duty to pass on messages upon which the fate of the entire battle may depend. Even for those of us long out of boot camp the binding burden remains: How are they to hear without the signal corpsman?

Considering this burden and these stammers, ought we not be a bit more cautious about our almost automatic advice to a young man: "Do not go into the ministry if you can possibly avoid it," recognizing that, at best, such advice is a half-truth. Of course there should be about the ordained vocation an urgency amounting almost to compulsion. But in point of fact there are countless and continuing ways to avoid it, in feckless faithlessness, in reckless flippancy, in careless disobedience, every day of a man's life. Looking back upon one's ordination day, more than once one will be moved to wonder why *that* day and how many more he can endure. Not infrequently he will come out of the pulpit and return to his home hardly able to break his fast, wondering whether what he is about is worth it all.

When that time comes, as come it will, I suggest that the spokesman for the Word pick up the second letter to the Corinthians, pondering particularly chapters 2 through 6, which James H. Robinson described as the "magnificent exposition of the preacher's task." In fact he will not need even to ponder it—just dip in and drink almost anywhere therein. And what will he find?

117

For we are the aroma of Christ to God among those who are being saved and among those who are perishing, to one a fragrance from death to death, to the other a fragrance from life to life. Who is sufficient for these things? For we are not, like so many, peddlers of God's word; but as men of sincerity, as commissioned by God, in the sight of God we speak in Christ. . . . Since we have such a hope, we are very bold. . . . Where the spirit of the Lord is, there is freedom. . . . We do not lose heart. . . . We refuse . . . to tamper with God's word, but by the open statement of the truth we would commend ourselves to every man's conscience in the sight of God. . . . But we have this treasure in earthen vessels, to show that the transcendent power belongs to God and not to us. . . . We are . . . perplexed, but not driven to despair; . . . and so we speak, knowing that he who raised the Lord Jesus will . . . bring us with you into his presence. . . . He who has prepared us for this very thing is God . . . . We must all appear before the judgment seat of Christ. . . . All this is from God, who through Christ reconciled us to himself and gave us the ministry of reconciliation. . . . So we are ambassadors for Christ, God making his appeal through us. (Cf. II Cor. 2–5.)

Yes, even through us, stammering but speaking the Word.

IV

Finally, both the *words* and the *Word* are intelligent and, in effective preaching, intelligible.

First, though, a warning which the preacher should really rivet to his imagination and memory. The famous dancer Anna Pavlova, after a particularly exhausting and demanding performance, was requested to interpret her meaning in words. She replied, "My God, do you think I would have danced it if I could have said it?" Some things cannot be said in words, though sometimes we are obliged, even with

118

the prior certainty of failure, to try. (That, by the way, is one of the practical reasons we should be grateful for the sacraments: What cannot be said can sometimes be done.) On the other hand, some things can be said in words. Douglas Horton calls a sacrament "what God employs to speak to us." [8] That is not definitive but it is helpful and descriptive of the sense in which we may speak of the sacrament of preaching. One of John Keble's hymns, with Jeremiah as its theme, contains the line, "My words are sacraments." Jeremiah himself thought so, as any prophet must:

"Behold, I am making my words in your mouth fire. . . . Thy words were found, and I ate them." (Jer. 5:14; 15:16.)
Words are by nature sacramental, outward expressions of inward truth.

Such a heightened value of words as I am here attempting to commend should not trick us into assuming that sermonic words are inevitably solemn. Decades ago R. W. Dale reminded us that the

traditional exclusion from the pulpit of humour and wit, dates from the worst and most artificial times of its history. The ancient preachers, the great preachers of the Middle Ages, the Puritan preachers, when they had the faculty, used it with wonderful effect. They did not think it necessary to be dull in order to be devout.[9]

I would put it more strongly still: When we have lost the capacity to laugh and therefore to laugh at ourselves, we have lost the capacity to perceive and embody the gospel. If Rein-

[8] *The Meaning of Worship*, p. 37.
[9] *The Ten Commandments* (New York: Eaton & Mains, n. d.), p. 74.

hold Niebuhr is right that laughter is the prelude to penitence, then a humorless people cannot even be authenically sad.

On the preacher's part, nevertheless, the price of intelligent and intelligible words is paid out in the currency of agony: hard labor nailed to a desk; holy supplication, kneeling in prayer. After due weight has been given to the limitations of spoken communications and to the impact of the communications revolution—Marshall McLuhan's *The Medium Is the Message,* and all the rest—I think we are not soon to see a wordless world. What we do have is a carelessly wordy world, and that because we are not willing to pay the price in care, in labor, in agony, to tell it like it is, choosing our words and phrasing our thoughts as if our very lives depended upon them, as indeed they do.

Clergymen are endemically subject to recurrent epidemics of hoof-and-mouth disease precisely because they talk so much, and must. The prescription is not silence (although a little of that would be nice now and then); the medicine is labor. In Calvin's Geneva, ministers were fined for intellectual laziness. Today we are more likely to reward them with ecclesiastical plums, permitting them the fruitless alibi that the other demands of the modern parish are so consuming (not to say consumptive) that they have no time to think.

Permit the poet to instruct and accuse us. T. S. Eliot has a marvelous passage in the "Four Quartets" in which he sings of just such agony of

> Trying to learn to use words, and every attempt
> Is a wholly new start, and a different kind of failure. . . .[10]

[10] *The Complete Poems and Plays* (New York: Harcourt, Brace & World, Inc., 1952), p. 128.

120

Then later:

> And every phrase
> And sentence that is right (where every word is at home,
> Taking its place to support the others,
> The word neither diffident nor ostentatious,
> An easy commerce of the old and the new,
> The common word exact without vulgarity,
> The formal word precise but not pedantic,
> The complete consort dancing together). . . .[11]

"My God," we might well exclaim, "do you think I would have said it if I could have danced it?" But that kind of dancing language is not won without daily rehearsal.

Moreover the intelligent and intelligible word of preaching is as simple as possible, but mind the qualifier. When people equate simple preaching with simpleminded preaching they are confusing simplicity with stupidity. One thing is worse than going over the people's heads, and that is to treat them as if they had no heads to go over. You may recall that sequence in Li'l Abner, back in the days before Al Capp had sold his satirical gifts to the cause of the *status quo*. Li'l Abner is arranging to sell his head to a scientist, on the off-chance that it might be the missing link the anthropologists are always looking for. Just before closing the deal, he says to the scientist, "My head's in good condition. I've never used it much." Some preachers have elevated that caption into a way of life. Some congregations have been perfectly content, in fact demonstrably relieved, to have them do so. One idiomatic expression neither preacher nor congregation can afford to admit to their lives together is: "Perish the thought."

[11] *Ibid.*, p. 144.

121

I delight in that story which comes out of the ministry of Bishop Francis J. McConnell. One of the ministers in a Conference over which the bishop was presiding was visibly perturbed at the church's thoughtlessness in electing a Ph.D., McConnell, to the episcopacy. He concluded his peroration from the floor of the Conference with these words, "Bishop, I am proud of my ignorance." To which the bishop is said to have replied, "Brother, you've got lots to be proud of!"

The obedient proclamation of the intelligent and intelligible Word obliges the church to be particularly on guard against that pious anti-intellectualism with which, in Protestantism at least, we are mightily supplied.

Words are not cheap. If they are, the Prologue to John's gospel is a cheap lie. Professor Merrill Abbey has called my attention to that moving scene in the Broadway play based upon the eloquent life of Helen Keller. Helen, a scared, trapped little almost-animal, is deaf and, as we so cruelly say, dumb. Ceaselessly and with an almost godly patience, Annie Sullivan, her companion, traces upon Helen's lips the tactile hints which, she prays, will one day break through to the Helen groaning to be released. Some day she *will* understand the relationship between the word "w-a-t-e-r" and the rushing fluid washing across the girl's hand from the pump. For, Annie says, "One word—and I could put the whole world in her hand."

Words are cheap we say? Only if we use them cheaply. The spoken sacrament is consecrated to the proposition that our human, humane, and humanizing words about the Word are called forth to be the instrument of his grace, the vessel of his truth, and the chalice of his glory, in us and in all men.

The most profoundly beautiful and beautifully profound definition of preaching I have ever read is provided by Theodore Parker Ferris in his helpful little volume, *Go Tell the People*. To preach, he says, is to draw aside the curtains from the figure of Christ, and to hide yourself in its folds. We do tolerably well drawing aside the curtains, not so well hiding ourselves in the folds. But it is worth a lifetime of effort, and requires a lifetime of devotion, to try.

[10]

THE WORLDLINESS OF
THE SACRAMENTS

To suggest that the church should be "worldly" would have been a scandalous assertion just a generation ago. That it is less so today is a mark of the church's progress in the direction of true self-knowledge.

God became man. God made a physical entrance into the world. And Christ lived out his life of union with the Father by loving the world and ultimately in giving himself totally for it. In the process he was branded by a self-righteous segment of people because he "ate with sinners"; he broke obsolete laws; he shocked the complacent; he became so totally "world" that Paul finally pointed out that he became totally like us in everything "except sin." And, as we remarked earlier, his presence is continuous, even now.

Surely he is present in the impressive pageantry of sacraments celebrated with all the ponderous dignity, awe, and precise correctness of many of our ritual enactments today. But that is because he agrees to be "all things to all men" and to be like us in everything but sin. However, the Christian church has been rather stodgy in meeting the contemporary world face-to-face. But he has stayed with us nonetheless, of course, even in such celebrations. But was such ponderous pageantry his way while physically on earth? No. He could have been rich but he chose to be poor. He could have had brass bands and "legions of angels," but he chose a donkey and the riffraff of the streets for his entry into Jerusalem. He was always simple and simply accessible, so that he could be understood by anyone who cared to receive his communications.

To communicate him; to assist him in making himself accessible to the whole world—this is *our* responsibility. I would say we have a good number of things to correct and refurbish; we have, as a matter of fact, an enormous amount of tearing down and rebuilding to do if we are to remain loyal to his essential intention.

If worship is the central meeting place of God, man, and community, the church is eternally faced with the responsibility of dealing with the symbols *of the day*. One of the church's most basic duties is keeping the symbol value relevant. This has assumed particular seriousness today, because modern man is quite skeptical of those symbols that are purported to be sacred. Partly this is because man has increasingly taken control of his own destiny and has learned he can regulate and govern things which a past age left completely in God's transcendent power. For example, he no longer worries about placating or beseeching God for all the rain he needs. He knows that he can now simply turn a switch and command irrigating waters in abundance. But partly also, the usefulness of some symbols can be questioned because the church has let them atrophy almost beyond the point of a general usefulness by not keeping them contemporary.

The first trend can be seen as a good one to the extent that it demolishes superstition; the latter can be seen only as an urgent reminder of our duty.

The contrast between the transcendent nature of God and human accomplishment and potential does not today propel man into the arms of an all-powerful deity as it did in the past. At most, religiously speaking, it places him in a situation where he must make a choice. And, unfortunately, we hinder the possibility of his choosing God because he cannot always see Christ. This is so because the "official" articulators of God have become complacent about changing his appearance, while the primary thing they are responsible for is keeping him fully recognizable to humanity in each succeeding age. That, of course, includes *this* age.

Sacramentality is the means by which each succeeding generation keeps in contact with God by discovering, celebrating, Christ's presence—his life, death, and resurrection today. We no longer speak the language of Chaucer, but we speak the same language more meaningfully because we keep our language up with the pace of life. This we must do in sacramental language for the active Christ among us. And it is *we* who must do it. Christ's presence and power are still operative among us by means of these various symbols in the midst of our living community. But we must speak our portion of this dialogue more intelligibly. We must speak as he did. More simply. Completely contemporaneously.

Sacraments and worship need to utilize objects, places, gestures, words, and actions that can symbolize Christ's life, passion, and resurrection as events alive and operative and constituent of the present community.

This all means that the sacraments must be *worldly*. The world is where we live. The secular sphere is no threat to

126

God's transcendence. It is the very stuff of which Christ's body is formed.

If we have outgrown the basically idolotrous mentality that found primitive cultures identifying holiness with certain objects and actions considered as sacred within themselves and as essentially distinct from profane objects, we have not grown sufficiently in faith to expect and assist the growth and change that is inevitably part of the life of a true body. And Christ has one!

We must recognize that it is useless to attempt to create an atmosphere of mystery in a liturgical celebration with symbols no longer mysterious. One wonders why we strive for mysteriousness anyway. The reality is mysterious enough; we should be making it intelligible. The mysteries of nature are no longer so mysterious. And, as one author has noted, aesthetic experience is largely questionable today as an apt vehicle, since the heights of architecture and art, polyphony, Gregorian chant, and such media are largely ineffectual, because they say nothing to the masses even though they may speak to the sophisticated. What would Christ do with the artifacts of today? This is not to disengage the value of art, but art's contribution must be increasingly contemporary and expressive of the religious-communal aspect it deals with.

Obviously the masses are not, in a day of demonstrations, riots, student protests, going to be deeply affected by any "triumphalism" no matter how condescending, since it makes the celebrant an authority figure in the mold of a royal person who is to be given humble and silent obeisance, a reflection of an older social order. Again, we must ask, what would Christ do?

The Second Vatican Council Document on the liturgy

says: "It is therefore of capital importance that the faithful easily understand the sacramental signs, and with great eagerness have frequent recourse to those sacraments which were instituted to nourish the Christian life." [1] This Council Document, as edited by Walter Abbot, has the following footnote to this statement: "Again the reiterated emphasis on intelligibility. Since the sacraments are there to 'nourish, strengthen, and express' faith and to give grace, they must be made as effective and fruitful as possible."

Where can we begin? We *can* use or refurbish the symbols we employ so that they relate more simply and directly to the saving events of Christ.

One suggestion for the process would be to note that contemporary man seems to be making an effort to be of service to the suffering, the weak, the afflicted. This, of course, is eminently Christ-like! Must not our symbols, then, contain an awareness and presence of suffering humanity? We must begin asking questions like:

How do you celebrate the Eucharist
 —on a hot, despairing evening in a sweltering, rat-infested slum?
 —in a complacent, facade-oriented suburb shopping center?

How do we bring the sacrament of reconciliation
 —to the people who live in a smoldering ruin after a riot, where they have looted, broken, destroyed?
 —to the distant landlords or antiseptically self-quarantined successful people, oblivious of the fact that they might be the cause of it?

[1] *The Documents of Vatican II,* "Liturgy," No. 59, p. 158.

What functional attire do we give confirmation in Christ
—to those bristling against injustice and about to fo-
ment a riot?
—but even more, to that protected, unconcerned Ameri-
cana that could prevent it if truly alive in Christ?

These and a million kindred questions call out for answer
to a church still more interested in polite polemics than incarnation.

What will we answer? For the answer is *ours* if God is to
become a human person and use us to give him contemporary
flesh.

The transition cannot take place all at once. But it must
vigorously begin. Pope John is a most fortunate illustration
of this point in a curious sort of fashion. As the beginner of a
transition himself, he still wore much of the traditional attire
of office. Yet, in reflecting upon it, one realizes that he did so
with a smile. He knew it was dated, but his saintly patience
caused him to begin to move into the new era, not throwing
bombs at everything of the past but reaching out to the future
with large feet planted consciously in the present, and permeated, permeated to the extent that the whole world knew it,
with love.

Let us close with a brief thought again on what really
underlies and enlivens all life in the church and her sacraments. What really totally permeates the whole of sacramental
life is the presence of Christ. Just that. And just that simply.
"He is risen and *is with us still.*" What special thing did the
apostles have when they ate with him? His presence. What
did the family at Bethany have when he was staying with
them? Him. When he died and his followers gathered, whose
presence made it essential that these disciples should gather

and pray? His. In the crowd of adults, whose hand did the child feel? His. Whom did Thomas need to touch? Him. After he left, whom did they sense intimately among them in the days of Pentecost? Him.

So he did not stop. He just kept on being there. And here. After his death, resurrection, ascension, his presence remained vitally there, as the essential catalyst that made the community different from other communities. They kept providing him physical means of expressing his presence among them, just as he had told them to do.

Are we doing as well?

We are doing it, but we are not doing it well. We can do it much better. We can do it so that he is more recognizable in our community of faith. We can do it if our faith is sufficiently alive to believe he can use our bodies, our gestures, actions, words, the places and things about us. We will do it best simply, with simple faith in the unbelievably simple way that God chose to communicate with us more fully. In a person. In him!

[afterword]

The granddaughter of Sir Edward Burne-Jones tells in her reminiscences how her grandfather, the nineteenth-century English painter and stained glass designer, put one of his art glass windows depicting the Holy Grail above the sink where the scullery maid labored for hours each day.

A chalice above the sink; a communion cup beside the water tap. That, we think and hope, is what this book is about.

We admit that often nothing appears as further removed from common life than our respective and sometimes similar liturgies. Few things seem more removed from the crush and crash of the everyday, from the push and pull of the ordinary.

Yet when Jesus indicated how he meant holiness to be shared, he did not select esoteric symbols. He took things that were signs of the everyday experiences of everyman and used them, particularly the bath and the burial which we call baptism, the common meal which we call the Eucharist. Holiness is not so much a matter of separation as of permeation. The chalice on the altar or table is a symbol of what we mean, but so is the tin cup on the town pump, by which I do not mean to suggest that the holy is common but rather that the common can be holy.

One of the early critical readers of these pages commented, at the request of the publishers: "The two men, . . . each departing from the main camps of sacramental theory that has in the past characterized their respective traditions, move to middle ground where they substantially agree. We do not, therefore, have a dialogue. There is too much agreement for that."

We do not know our critic, but we are grateful to him. He thus confirms our point, our purpose, and our expectations. One of the marvelous, moving, and surprising discoveries we made as we set about to prepare these pages was that the doctrinal distance between us, sacramentally, is far less than we had anticipated. In all truth, "let us give thanks unto the Lord."

Not that our or anybody's language is adequate to express either consensus or conflict. If contemporary linguistic philosophy has taught us anything, it is that theological language is first language, purposeful though imprecise, and only after that is it theology.[1] Theological discourse partakes of all the limping inexactitude and rapid eloquence which any word usage requires and involves.

Another thing the two of us have learned from each other and from our thoughtful confreres is the urgency of the questions which press upon us a consideration of what it means to be Christian in our time; we have especially tried to say what the sacraments contribute to those questions. But the human inquiry undergirds the whole.

In one of the groups we invited to respond and poke holes in this literary theological effort was a young law student, Kent

[1] See Chap. II, p. 30.

Hull. He commented that, as a Christian, he has a habit of roughly dividing the books he reads into those intended for "insiders" and those meant for "outsiders." He added that, in the case of the present volume, he had difficulty making such a distinction with any certainty. Once more, we are gratified. We like to think that what we have written addresses Christians and addresses them where they live, where they think, feel, are. But hopefully some of what we have thought and written here will commend itself to those who claim no such label and name no such Lord. They may call themselves "humanists." (They may be surprised to learn that we do, too, in our more thoughtful, less institutional moments.) They may disclaim all labels. (That we can understand. Frankly labels no longer excite, upset, or even greatly interest us.) But if even one of our chapters makes a bit clearer what it means to be fully human, then, we contend, our effort has found one of its important targets.

We would not want our joint satisfaction with our critic's comment ("we do not . . . have a dialogue") to obscure the fact that important points of doctrinal difference remain. As we reread what we have written, it is clear to us that we may not have done justice to such questions as these:

(1) What is baptismal regeneration? What is meant by original sin? How do these two notions square with what we have asserted about the sacrament of baptism?

(2) When we authors unite to affirm the real presence of Christ in the sacrament of the Eucharist, is each of us using the word "presence" or the word "real" in the same sense?

(I, the Protestant partner, must here record a moment of genuine spiritual enlightenment when I heard my Roman brother say that what Christ has given us in the Holy Meal is his Presence; what the theologians had given us, for perfectly

133

understandable and reasonably adequate historical reasons, was an *explanation* of that Presence. Then, repeating this distinction, he added softly, "I'll stay with what the Lord gave us.")

(3) When we two authors use the word "sacrifice" in relation to the Eucharist, again, are we using that word with a common meaning? Are we covering or covering up our differences? (Here I, the Protestant partner, confess that I think my usage of the word has been most fragmented, partial, and inadequate, while the Catholic partner rejoices that the word is such a viable common instrument of discussion on this doctrinal point.)

In the midst of the correspondence which led to the lectureship upon which this book is based, we were requested to conduct jointly a service of Holy Communion. Conceivably we could have attempted such a service. We could have devised some "demonstration liturgy" (terrible term!). We could have confused (or worse, misled) our ecclesiastical superiors. We could have imagined a unity which did not yet (quite) exist. However, we decided that it would be more honest to decline to force or fake our unity. The sacramental sign of unity must be treated honestly and reverently, we felt. We concluded that it would be better to require once again the experience of the painful recognition that we have not yet achieved all those practical forms of unity without which our true unity is fractured and unreal. We personally regretted this necessity. It gave us pain. But it also seemed necessary. Therefore we were resolute about it.

Another point at which the spark of insight leapt the gap of doctrine was in our separate but astonishingly unified conclusions about the "lost sacraments" (from the Protestant perspective), or the "other five" (from the Roman Catholic viewpoint). We discovered (and told each other, to our mutual relief and enlightenment) that (1) Protestants either observe these in some form or have neglected them to their impoverishment, and that (2) Catholics observe seven sacraments but do not accord them equal importance; that the latter have in practice, and probably in principle, a hierarchy of sacraments. This being so, only the desire to play theological games, pushing doctrinal pawns and bishops around for intellectual excitement, will cause us to weight *that* debate with crucial importance. We need, and are determined, to get on with it.

Our concluding discussion of the worldliness of the sacraments participates in the current interest in the category of the secular, although not (we hope) as a theological catchword or fad. It involves something at once more profound and simple than that, something we may not have quite succeeded in expressing. Perhaps it is impossible to do so propositionally.

The mechanism of indirect discourse may say it, or at least suggest it, more adequately. The Italian novelist Ignazio Silone, called "unbelieving" by some, captures the tone of our intent in his book *Bread and Wine*. In one subdued but climactic scene, family and friends have gathered in the boyhood home of a young revolutionary who has been subjected to a cruel and humiliating death: chamber pot on his head, broom in his hand, kicked to death by the militia. The talk quite naturally turns to remembrances of what Luigi had said and done during his few years. A simple meal is laid out upon the rustic table. Then the boy's father speaks:

"It was he who helped to sow, to weed, to thresh, to mill the grain from which this bread was made. Take it and eat it; this is his bread."

Some others arrived. The father gave them something to drink and said, "It was he who helped me to prune, to spray, to weed and to harvest the grapes which went into this wine. Drink; this is his wine." . . .

Some beggars arrived. "Let them in," said the mother.[2]

Now long ago a Protestant minister was invited by a Catholic priest to preach at Mass. In the homily before the post-communion hymn, he spoke of the agony of our divisions as Christians. Later in the service he was invited to stand with his Catholic brothers around the altar as the celebration proceeded. When it came time to serve communion, both priest and pastor were uneasy and, for an instant, embarrassed. The Protestant did not receive the Host.

Immediately, however, the priest stepped to the altar and said, "Beloved in the Lord, we have participated this day in a demonstration of both our unity and our disunity in Christ. A brother in Christ has broken for us the Bread of Life. Yet because of a regulation of the Church he has not been permitted to receive the Holy Communion. Let each of us go out from this place determined to labor in love for the removal of what he has called the agony of our disunity."

That event, the unity and disunity it embodies and declares, expresses where we are. We both rejoice in the unity and feel equally responsible for the disunity. And on that note we conclude this experiment in ecumenical honesty—with profound regret, and profounder hope.

[2] Ignazio Silone, *Bread and Wine* (New York: The New American Library, 1963), p. 269.

[selected bibliography]

A. Books

Aquinas, St. Thomas. *Summa Theologica*. Trans. of the Engl. Dominican Province. New York: Benziger Brothers, 1948.

Baillie, D. M. *The Theology of the Sacraments*. New York: Charles Scribner's Sons, 1957.

Bruce, Robert. *The Mystery of the Lord's Supper*. London: J. Clarke, 1958.

Constitution on the Church of Vatican Council II. The Missionary Society of St. John the Apostle in the State of New York, Glen Rock, N. J.: Paulist Press, 1965.

Consultation on Church Union. The Executive Committee on the Consultation on Church Union for the Biennium 1966-68. Cincinnati, Ohio: Forward Movement Publication, 1967.

Clark, Francis. *Eucharistic Sacrifice and the Reformation*. Westminster, Md.: Newman Press, 1961.

Diekmann, Godfrey. *Come, Let Us Worship*. Garden City, N. Y.: Image Books, 1966.

Edwall, Pehr, *et al.*, eds. *Ways of Worship: The Report of a Theological Commission of Faith and Order*. Harper & Bros., 1951.

Hardin, H. G., Quillian, J. D., Jr., and White, J. F. *The Celebration of the Gospel*. Nashville: Abingdon Press, 1964.

Kennedy, Eugene C. *Fashion Me a People: Man, Woman, and the Church*. New York: Sheed & Ward, 1967.

Marty, Martin E. *Baptism*. Philadelphia: Fortress Press (Muhlenberg Press), 1962.

137

New Catechism, A Catholic Faith for Adults. The higher Catechetical Institute at Nigmegen. Trans. by Kevin Smyth. New York: Herder and Herder, 1967.

Pastoral Constitution on the Church in the Modern World. Text of an English trans. relayed from Vatican City to the Press Dept. of the National Catholic Welfare Conference, Washington, D.C. Huntington, Ind.: Our Sunday Visitor, n.d.

Pope Paul VI. *Constitution on the Sacred Liturgy of the Second Vatican Council and the motu proprio.* Study Club Ed., The Missionary Society of St. Paul the Apostle in the State of New York. Glen Rock, N. J.: Paulist Press, 1964.

Phifer, Kenneth G. *A Protestant Case for Liturgical Renewal.* Philadelphia: Westminster Press, 1965.

Rahner, Karl. *The Church and the Sacraments.* New York: Herder and Herder, 1963.

Rattenbury, John Ernest. *The Eucharistic Hymns of John and Charles Wesley.* London: Epworth Press, 1948.

Robinson, John A. T. *Liturgy Coming to Life.* Philadelphia: Westminster Press, 1964.

Schillebeeckx, Edward, and Willems, Boniface, eds. *The Sacraments in General, a New Perspective.* Glen Rock, N. J.: Paulist Press, 1968.

——————— *Christ the Sacrament of the Encounter with God.* New York: Sheed & Ward, 1963.

Semmelroth, Otto, S.J. *Church and Sacraments.* Notre Dame, Ind.: Fides Publishers, 1965.

Temple, William. *Nature, Man and God.* New York: The Macmillan Co., 1949.

Todd, John M. *John Wesley and the Catholic Church.* London: Hodder & Stroughton, 1952.

Wesley, John. *Standard Sermons.* 2 vols. Sugden, E. H., ed. Naperville, Ill.: Allenson, 3rd. ed., 1921.

Winward, Stephen F. *The Reformation of Our Worship.* Richmond, Va.: John Knox Press, 1965.

Swidler, Leonard J., ed. *Ecumenism, the Spirit, and Worship.* Pittsburgh: Duquesne University Press, 1967.

B. ARTICLES

Baum, Gregory. "Liturgy and Unity," *Ecumenist,* V (November-December, 1967).

Brändle, Max. "Narratives of the Synoptics About the Tomb," *Theology Digest*, XVI (Spring, 1968).

Brown, Raymond E. "The Resurrection and Biblical Criticism," *Commonweal*, LXXXVII (November 24, 1967).

Clarke, Tomas E. "The Humanity of Jesus," *Commonweal*, LXXXVII (November 24, 1967).

Dupré, Louis. "Religion in a Secular World," *Christianity and Crisis*, XXVII (April 15, 1968).

Fiedler, Ernest. "The Idea of Worship," Pontifical Gregorian University, Rome, 1952.

———— "From 'Discovery of Liturgy to Creative Renewal,'" IDO-C doss 67-35 (October 15, 1967).

———— "From the Point of View of the Expression of the Faith," IDO-C doss 67-34 (October 12, 1967).

Hafnew, George J. "A New Style of Christianity," *Commonweal*, LXXXVIII (May 31, 1968).

———— "Historical Sense," *Duckett's Register*, XXII (December, 1967).

Lepargneur, Francis, H. "The Place of a Sick Person in a Christian Anthropology," *Theology Digest*, VI (Summer, 1968).

McSorley, Harry J. "Protestant Eucharistic Reality and Lack of Orders," *Ecumenist* (July-August, 1967).

Murphy-O'Connor, Jerome. "Sin and Community in the New Testament, *Theology Digest*, VI (Summer, 1968).

O'Neill, Colman. "The Recipient and Sacramental Signification," *Theology Digest*, II (Autumn, 1964).

Porter, H. Boone, Jr. "Baptism: In Paschal and Ecumenical Setting," *Worship*, XLII (April, 1968).

———— "Two ways of Viewing the 'Liturgy of the Church,'" IDO-C doss 67-35 (October 15, 1967).

Vawter, Bruce. "The Johannine Sacramentary, *Theology Digest*, VI (Winter, 1958).

Weakland, Robert G. "Worship in a Secular World," IDO-C doss 68-11 (March 17, 1968).

Wedel, Theodore O. "Is Preaching Outmoded?" *Religion in Life*, XXXIV (Autumn, 1965), 534-47.

Yeomans, William. "The Essential Eucharist," *Duckett's Register*, XIV (May, 1968).

[index]

Incarnation, 53
  communication of, 26
  new meaning of, 26-27
Isaiah, 12, 13

Janes, Bishop Edmund S., 115
Jesus
  baptism of, 34
  communications of, 125
  sacrament of, 16
  simplicity of, 125
John
  letter of, 75-76
  gospel of, 24
  XXIII, Pope, on sacrifice, 68, 110

Keller, Helen, 122

Language
  inadequacies of, 31
  mystery of, 31
Leacock, Stephen, 87
Leo I, Pope, 45
Leeming, Bernard, 89
Lombard, Peter, 87-88
Luther, 19, 105

Marriages, mixed, 71
Marty, Martin E., 44-46
Matrimony
  Christ's presence in, 96, 101
  malpractice of, 94
McConnell, Frances J., 122
McLuhan, Marshall, 120
Metaphysics, Christian, 21
Michalson, Carl, 38
Ministry, burdens of, 117
Mystery
  needs for, 15, 20, 30, 76
  relation of, to sacramentals, 15
  redemptive, 76
  theological study of, 30

Old Testament
  meaning of, 68
  revelation recorded in, 28, 68

Ontology, Christian, 21
Ordination, 96
Original sin, 20

Paul, the apostle, 29, 33, 107, 110
Penance, 90, 120
  cleansing in, 20
Pentecost, 54
Phifer, Kenneth G., 63
Philosophy, linguistic, 132
Porter, H. B., 53-54
Preaching
  tension of, 114
  definition of, by Theodore Parker
    Ferris, 123
Presence
  gestures of, 17
  in word, 17
  need for, 15, 20
Priesthood
  universal, 71
  validation of, 71
Protestantism, 65
  lack of Penance, 90
  lack of uniformity, 97
  since Reformation, 30
Puritan, 60

Radbertus, Paschasius, 62
Rahner, Karl, 102
Ratramnus, 63
Redemption, 15
  grace of, 16
Reformers, 63
Regeneration, baptismal, 133
Revelation, of God, 28
Ritual, 124
Roman Catholicism since Reformation, 30
Rupp, Gordon, 67

Sacramental theology, 89
Sacraments
  as symbols, 29, 85
  definition of, 16, 85, 89, 119
  encounter with Christ, 16